HERE
THERE BE
DRAGONS

Jane Yolen

HERE THERE BE DRAGONS

Illustrated by DAVID WILGUS

HARCOURT BRACE & COMPANY

San Diego   New York   London

"Great-Grandfather Dragon's Tale" by Jane Yolen previously
appeared in *Dragons and Dreams* by Jane Yolen, Martin H. Greenberg,
and Charles G. Waugh, copyright © 1986 by Jane Yolen,
Martin H. Greenberg, and Charles G. Waugh, published by
HarperCollins Publishers. "The King's Dragon" by Jane Yolen
previously appeared in *Spaceships and Spells* by Jane Yolen,
Martin H. Greenberg, and Charles G. Waugh, copyright © 1987
by Jane Yolen, Martin H. Greenberg, and Charles G. Waugh,
published by HarperCollins Publishers. Reprinted by permission.

Library of Congress Cataloging-in-Publication Data
Yolen, Jane.
Here there be dragons/by Jane Yolen; illustrated
by David Wilgus.—1st ed.
p.   cm.
Summary: A collection of both new and previously
published stories and poems about dragons by Jane Yolen.
ISBN 0-15-209888-7
1. Dragons—Literary collections.   2. Children's literature,
American.   [1. Dragons—Literary collections.   2. Literature—
Collections.   3. Fairy tales.   4. Fantasy.   5. Short stories.
6. American poetry.]   I. Wilgus, David, ill.   II. Title.
PZ7.Y78Hi   1993
[Fic]—dc20   92-23194

Designed by Camilla Filancia
B C D E

Printed in the United States of America

For Erica St. George,

by name and by nature

a dragon tamer

—J. Y.

Contents

HERE THERE BE DRAGONS

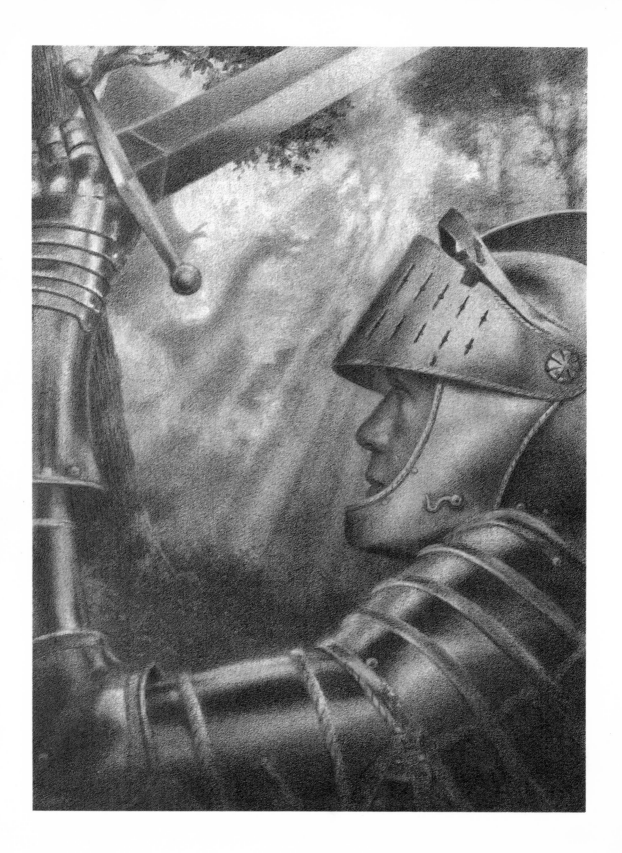

Ursula Le Guin once remarked that we shouldn't banish dragons from our literature—as some fanatics would have us do—because then we banish the possibility of Saint George. I was thinking about that while reading a description by Georgess McHargue of the encounter between the sword-wielding saint and the mighty Wyrm in her wonderful book The Beasts of Never.

Before I knew it, I was writing this bit of verse. It was a cold December, but the heat of the forging of this particular poem, over several days, kept me quite warm.

Why Dragons?

The smoke still hangs heavily over the meadow,
Circling down from the mouth of the cave,
While kneeling in prayer, full armored and haloed,
The lone knight is feeling uncertainly brave.

The promise of victory sung in the churches,
Is hardly a murmur out here in the air.
All that he hears is the thud of his faint heart
Echoing growls of the beast in its lair.

The steel of his armor would flash in the sunlight,
Except that the smoke has quite hidden the sky.
The red of the cross on his breast should sustain him,
Except—he suspects—it's a perfect bull's-eye.

The folk of the village who bet on the outcome
Have somehow all fled from the scene in dismay.

1

They'll likely return in a fortnight or longer,
He doubts that they'll be of much help on this day.

And then—with a scream—the fell beast of the cavern
Flings its foul body full out of the cave.
The knight forgets prayers and churches and haloes
And tries to remember just how to be brave.

The webs on the wings of the dragon are reddened,
With blood or with sunlight, the knight is not sure.
The head of the beast is a silver-toothed nightmare,
Its tongue drips a poison for which there's no cure.

He thrusts with his sword and he pokes with his gauntlets,
He knees with his poleyn, kicks out with his greave.
He'd happily give all the gold in his pocket
If only the dragon would quietly leave.

There's smoke and there's fire, there's wind and there's growling,
There's screams from the knight, and his sobs and his cries.
And when the smoke clears, there's the sound of dry heaving
As one of the two of them messily dies.

Of course it's the knight who has won this hard battle,
Who wins in a poem beaten out on a forge
Of human devising and human invention.
BUT:
       If there's no dragon—then there's no Saint George.

There are many famous dragon stories from the point of view of the dragon-slayer. But one day I began to think that the dragons might have a very different idea about what happened. And if it got told over and over, down through the years, that dragon story could have the power of legend to the scaly set.

Wyrm *is the old word for dragon. It comes from Old English.*

Great-Grandfather Dragon's Tale

1.

"Long, long ago," said the old dragon, and the gray smoke curled around his whiskers in thin, tired wisps, "in the time of the Great-Grandfather of All Dragons, there was no Thanksgiving."

The five little dragons looked at one another in alarm. The boldest of them, Sskar, said, "No Thanksgiving? No feasting? No chestnuts on the fire? Hasn't there always been a Thanksgiving?"

The old dragon wheezed. The smoke came out in huge, alarming puffs. Then he started speaking, and the smoke resumed its wispy rounds. "For other animals, perhaps. For rabbits or lions or deer. Perhaps for them there has always been a Thanksgiving."

"Rabbits and lions and deer!" The little dragons said the names with disdain. And Sskar added, "Who cares about rabbits and lions and deer. We want to know about dragons!"

"Then listen well, young saurs. For what was once could come again. What was then could be now. And once there was no dragons' Thanksgiving."

The little dragons drew closer, testing their claws against the stone floor of the cave, and listened.

Long, long ago *began the old dragon* the world was ice and fire, fire and ice. In the south, great mountains rained smoke and spat flame.

3

In the north, glaciers like beasts crept down upon the land and devoured it.

It was then that the Great-Grandfather of All Dragons lived.

He was five hundred slithes from tip to tail. His scales shimmered like the moon on waves. His eyes were black shrouds. He breathed fire storms, which he could fan to flame with his mighty wings. And his feet were broad enough to carry him over the thundering miles. All who saw him were afraid.

And the Great-Grandfather of All Dragons ate up the shaking fear of the little animals. He lived on it and thrived. He would roar and claw and snatch and hit about with his tail just to watch fear leap into the eyes of the watchers. He was mighty, yet he was just one of many, for in those days dragons ruled the earth.

One day, up from the south, from the grassy lands, from the sweet lands, where the red sun pulls new life from the abundant soil, a new creature came. He was smaller than the least of the dragons, not even a slithe and a half high. He had no claws. His teeth were puny and blunt. He could breathe neither fire nor smoke, and he had neither armor to protect himself nor fur to keep himself warm. His legs could only carry him from here—to there. *And the old dragon drew a small line on the rockface with his littlest toenail.*

But when he opened his mouth, the sounds of all beasts, both large and small, of the air and the sea and the sky came out. It was this gift of sound that would make him the new king.

"Fah!" said little Sskar. "How could something that puny be a king? The only sound worth making more than once or twice is this." And he put his head back and roared. It was a small roar, for he was still a small dragon, but little as it was, it echoed for miles and caused three trees to wither on the mountain's face. True, they were stunted trees that had weathered too many storms and were

above the main tree line. But they shivered at the sound, dropped all their remaining leaves, and died where they stood.

The other little dragons applauded the roar, their claws clacketting together. And one of them, Sskitter, laughed. Her laugh was delicate and high pitched, but she could roar as loudly as Sskar.

"Do not laugh at what you do not understand," said the old dragon. "Look around. What do you see? We are few, yet this new creature is many. We live only in this hidden mountain wilderness while he and his children roam the rest of the world. We glide on shrunken wings over our shrunken kingdom while he flies in great silver birds all over the earth."

"Was it not always so?" asked the smallest dragon, Sskarma. She was shaken by the old one's words.

"No, it was not always so," said the old dragon.

"Bedtime," came a soft voice from the corner. Out from behind a large rock slithered Mother Dragon. "Settle down, my little firetongues. And you, Grandfather, no more of that story for this night."

"Tomorrow?" begged Sskarma, looking at the old one.

He nodded his mighty head, and the smoke made familiar patterns around his horns.

As they settled down, the little dragons listened while their mother and the old one sang them a lullaby:

Firelight and firebright,
Bank your dragon flames tonight.
Close your eyes and still your roar,
Sleep is here, my little saur.
Hiss, hiss, hush.

By the time the song was over, all but little Sskar had dropped off. He turned around and around on the cave floor, trying to get settled. "Fah!" he muttered to himself. "What kind of king is that?" But at last he, too, was asleep, dreaming of bones and fire.

5

"Do not fill their heads with nonsense," said Mother Dragon when the hatchlings were quiet.

"It is not nonsense," said the old dragon. "It is history."

"It is dreams," she retorted. In her anger, fire shot out of her nostrils and singed the old one's nose. "If it cannot feed their bellies, it is worthless. Good night, Grandfather." She circled her body around the five little dragons and, covering them, slept.

The old dragon looked at the six of them long after the cave was silent. Then he lay down with his mouth open facing the cave entrance as he had done ever since he had taken a mate. He hardly slept at all.

2.

In the morning, the five little dragons were up first, yawning and hissing and stretching. They sharpened their claws on the stone walls, and Sskar practiced breathing smoke. None of the others was even close to smoke yet. Most were barely trickling straggles through their nose slits.

It was midmorning before Grandfather Dragon moved. He had been up most of the night thinking, checking the wind currents for scents, keeping alert for dangerous sounds carried on the air. When morning had come, he had moved away from the cave mouth and fallen asleep. When Grandfather awoke it was in sections. First his right foreleg moved, in short hesitations as if testing its flexibility. Then his left. Then his massive head moved from side to side. At last he thumped his tail against the far rocks of the cave. It was a signal the little dragons loved.

Sskarma was first to shout it out. "The story! He is going to tell us the story!" She ran quickly to her grandfather and curled around his front leg, sticking her tail into her mouth. The others took up their own special positions and waited for him to begin.

"And what good was this gift of sound?" asked the old dragon at last, picking up the tale as if a night and half a day had not come between tellings.

"What good?" asked the little dragons. Sskar muttered, "What good indeed?" over and over until Sskitter hit him on the tip of the nose with a claw.

This gift of sound *said Grandfather Dragon* which made the creature king, could be used in many ways. He could coax the birds and beasts into his nets by making the sound of a hen calling the cock or a lioness seeking the lion or a bull elk spoiling for a fight. And so cock and lion and bull elk came. They came at this mighty hunter's calling, and they died at his hand.

Then the hunter learned the sounds that a dragon makes when he is hungry. He learned the sounds that a dragon makes when he is sleepy, when he looks for shelter, calls out warning, seeks a mate. All these great sounds of power the hunter learned—and more. And so one by one the lesser dragons came at his calling; one by one they came—and were killed.

The little dragons stirred uneasily at this. Sskarma shivered and put her tail into her mouth once more.

So we dragons named him *Ssgefah*, which, in the old tongue, means "enemy." But he called himself Man.

"Man," they all said to one another. "Ssgefah. Man."

At last one day the Great-Grandfather of All Dragons looked around and saw that there were only two dragons left in the whole world—he and his mate. The two of them had been very cunning and had hidden themselves away in a mountain fastness, never answering any call but a special signal that they had planned between themselves.

"I know that signal," interrupted Sskitter. She gave a shuddering, hissing fall of sound.

The old dragon smiled at her, showing 147 of his secondary teeth. "You have learned it well, child. But do not use it in fun. It is the most powerful sound of all."

The little dragons all practiced the sound under their breaths while the old dragon stretched and rubbed an itchy place under his wing.

7

"Supper!" hissed Mother Dragon, landing on the stone outcropping by the cave mouth. She carried a mountain goat in her teeth. But the little dragons ignored her.

"Tell the rest," pleaded Sskarma.

"Not the rest," said the old dragon, "but I will tell you the next part."

3.

"We must find a young Man who is unarmed," said the Great-Grandfather of All Dragons. "One who has neither net nor spear."

"And *eat* him!" said his mate. "It has been such a long time since we have had any red meat. Only such grasses and small birds as populate tops of mountains. It is dry, ribey fare at best." She yawned prettily and showed her sharp primary teeth.

"No," said the Great-Grandfather of All Dragons. "We shall capture him and learn his tongue. And then we will seal a bargain between us."

His mate looked shocked. Her wings arched up; great ribbed wings they were, too, with the skin between the ribbings as bright as blood. "A bargain? With such a puny thing as Man?"

The Great-Grandfather of All Dragons laughed sadly then. It was a dry, deep, sorrowful chuckle. "Puny?" he said, as quietly as smoke. "And what are we?"

"Great!" she replied, staring black eye into black eye. "Magnificent. Tremendous. Awe inspiring." She stood and stretched to her fullest, which was 450 slithes in length. The mountaintop trembled underneath her magnificently ponderous legs.

"You and I," said the Great-Grandfather of All Dragons, "and who else?"

She looked around, saw no other dragons, and was still.

"Why, that's just what you said last night, Grandfather," said little Sskitter.

Grandfather Dragon patted her on the head. *"Good girl. Bright girl. Perceptive girl."*

Sskar drew his claws lazily over the floor of the cave, making awful squeaks and leaving scratches in the stone. *"I knew that,"* he said. Then he blew smoke rings to show he did not care that his sister had been praised.

But the other dragons were not afraid to show they cared. *"I remember,"* said Ssgrum.

"Me, too," said Sstok.

They both came in for their share of praises.

Sskarma was quiet and stared. Then she said, *"But more story, Grandfather."*

"First comes supper," said Mother Dragon. *"Growing bodies need to eat."*

This time they all listened.

But when there was not even a smidgen of meat left, and only the bones to gnaw and crack, Mother Dragon relented.

"Go ahead now," she said. *"Tell them a story. But no nonsense."*

"This is true history," said Sskitter.

"It's dumb!" said Sskar. He roared his roar again. *"How could there be us if they were the last of the dragons?"*

"It's a story," said Sskarma. *"And a story should be its own reward. I want to hear the rest."*

The others agreed. They settled down again around Grandfather Dragon's legs, except for Sskar, who put his back against the old dragon's tail. That way he could listen to the story but pretend not to be interested.

4.

So the Great-Grandfather of All Dragons *the story began once more* flew that very night on silent wings, setting them so that he could glide and catch the currents of air. And he was careful not to roar or to breathe fire or to singe a single tree.

He quartered town after town, village after village, farm after farm, all fitted together as carefully as puzzles. And at last he came

9

to a young shepherd boy asleep beside his flock out in a lonely field.

The Great-Grandfather of All Dragons dropped silently down at the edge of the field, holding his smoke so that the sheep—silly creatures—would not catch the scent of him. For dragons, as you know, have no odor other than the brimstone smell of their breath. The black-and-white sheepdog with the long hair twitched once, as if the sound of the Great-Grandfather's alighting had jarred his sleep, but he did not awaken.

Then the Great-Grandfather of All Dragons crept forward slowly, trying to sort out the sight and sound and smell of the youngling. He seemed to be about twelve Man years old and unarmed except for his shepherd's staff. He was fair haired and had a sprinkling of spots over the bridge of his nose that Men call freckles. He wore no shoes and smelled of cheese and bread, slightly moldy. There was also a green smell coming from his clothes, a tree and grass and rain and sun smell, which the Great-Grandfather of All Dragons liked.

The boy slept a very deep sleep. He slept so deeply because he thought that the world was rid of dragons, that all he had to worry about were wolves and bears and the sharp knife of hunger. Yes, he believed that dragons were no more until he dreamed them and screamed—and woke up, still screaming, in a dragon's claw.

Sskar applauded. "I like the part about the dragon's claw," he said, looking down at his own golden nails.

Sskitter poked him with her tail, and he lashed back. They rolled over and over until the old dragon separated them with his own great claws. Only then did they settle down to listen.

But when he saw that screaming would not help, the young Man stopped screaming, for he was very brave for all that he was very young.

11

And when he was set down in the lair and saw he could not run off because the dragon's mate had blocked the door, the young Man made a sign against his body with his hand and said, "Be gone, Worm." For that is how Man speaks.

"Be gone, Worm," Sskitter whispered under her breath.

And Sskarma made the Man sign against her own body, head to heart, shoulder to shoulder. It did not make sense to her, but she tried it anyway.

Sskar managed to look amused, and the two younger dragons shuddered.

"Be gone, Worm," the Manling said again. Then he sat down on his haunches and cried, for he was a very young Man after all. And the sound of his weeping was not unlike the sound of a baby dragon calling for its food.

At that, the Great-Grandmother of All Dragons moved away from the cave mouth and curled herself around the Man and tried to comfort him, for she had no hatchlings of her own yet, though she had wished many years for them. But the Man buffeted her with his fist on the tender part of her nose, and she cried out in surprise—and in pain. Her roar filled the cave. Even the Great-Grandfather closed his earflaps. And the young Man held his hands up over the sides of his face and screamed back. It was not a good beginning.

But at last they both quieted down, and the Manling stretched out his hand toward the tender spot and touched it lightly. And the Great-Grandmother of All Dragons opened her second eyelid—another surprise—and the great fires within her eyes flickered.

It was then that the Great-Grandfather of All Dragons said quietly in dragon words, "Let us begin."

The wonder of it was that the young Man understood.

"My name," he replied in Man talk, in a loud, sensible voice, "is Georgi." He pointed to himself and said "Georgi" again.

The Great-Grandfather of All Dragons tried. He said "Ssgggi," which we have to admit was not even close.

The Great-Grandmother of All Dragons did not even try.

So the youngling stood and walked over, being careful not to make any sudden gestures, and pointed straight at the Great-Grandfather's neck.

"Sskraken," roared the Great-Grandfather, for as you know a dragon always roars out his own name.

"Sskar!" roared Sskar, shattering a nearby tree. A small, above-the-frost-line tree. The others were silent, caught up in the story's spell.

And when the echo had died away, the youngling said in a voice as soft as the down on the underwing of an owl, "Sskraken." He did not need to shout it to be heard, but every syllable was there. It made the Great-Grandfather shiver. It made the Great-Grandmother put her head on the floor and think.

"Sskraken," the youngling said again, nodding as if telling himself to remember. Then he turned to Sskraken's mate and pointed at her. And the pointing finger never trembled.

"Sskrema," she said, as gently as a lullaby. It was the first time in her life that she had not roared out her name.

The youngling walked over to her, rubbed the spot on her nose that had lately been made sore. "Sskrema," he crooned. And to both their astonishments, she thrummed under his hand.

"She thrummed!" said Sskitter. "But you have told us . . ."

"Never to thrumm except to show the greatest happiness with your closest companions," the youngest two recited dutifully.

"So I did," said Grandfather Dragon. With the tip of his tail, he brushed away a fire-red tear that was caught in his eye. But he did it cleverly, so cleverly the little dragons did not notice. "So I did."

13

"Fah!" said Sskar. "It was a mistake. All a mistake. She never would have thrummed knowingly at a Man."

"That's what makes it so important," answered Sskarma. She reached up with her tail and flicked another tear from the old dragon's eye, but so cleverly the others never noticed. Then she thrummed at him. "Tell us more."

5.

The youngling Georgi lived with the two saurs for a year and a day. He learned many words in the old tongue: *sstek* for red meat and *sstik* for the dry, white meat of birds; *ssova*, which means "egg," and *ssouva*, which means "soul." Learning the old tongue was his pleasure, his task, and his gift.

In return, the Great-Grandfather of All Dragons and his mate learned but one word. It was the name of the Man—Georgi. Or as they said it, "Ssgggi."

At the end of the year and a day, the Great-Grandfather called the boy to him, and they walked away from the sweet-smelling nest of grasses and pine needles and attar of wild rose that Georgi had built for them. They walked to the edge of the jagged mountainside where they could look down on the rough waste below.

"Ssgggi," said the Great-Grandfather of All Dragons, speaking the one word of Man's tongue he had learned, though he had never learned it right. "It is time for you to go home. For though you have learned much about us and much from us, you are not a dragon but a Man. Now you must take your learning to them, the Men, and talk to them in your own Man's tongue. Give them a message from us. A message of peace. For if you fail, we who are but two will be none." And he gave a message to the Man.

Georgi nodded and then quietly walked back to the cave. At his footsteps, the Great-Grandmother of All Dragons appeared. She looked out and stared at the boy. They regarded one another solemnly, without speaking. In her dark eyes the candle flame flickered.

"I swear that I will not let that light go out," said Georgi, and he rubbed her nose. And then they all three thrummed at one another, though the Man did it badly.

Then he turned from the saurs without a further good-bye. And this was something else he had learned from the Great-Grandfather, for Men tend to prolong their good-byes, saying meaningless things instead of leaping swiftly into the air.

"It is their lack of wings," said Sskarma thoughtfully.

Georgi started down the mountain, the wind in his face and a great roar at his back. The mountains shook at his leaving, and great boulders shrugged down the cliff sides. And high above him, the two saurs circled endlessly in the sky, guarding him though he knew it not.

And so the Manling went home and the dragons waited.

"Dragons have a long patience," the two youngest saurs recited dutifully. "That is their genius." And when no one applauded their memories, they clattered their own claws together and smiled at one another, toothy smiles, and slapped their tails on the stone floor.

6.

In dragon years *continued Grandfather Dragon* it was but an eyelid's flicker, though in Man years it was a good long while.

And then one day, when the bright eye of the sun was for a moment shuttered by the moon's dark lid, a great army of Men appeared at the mouth of the canyon and rode their horses almost to the foot of the mountain.

The Great-Grandmother of All Dragons let her rough tongue lick around her jaws at the sight of so much red meat.

15

"*Sstek,*" she said thoughtfully.

But the Great-Grandfather cautioned her, remembering how many dragons had died in fights with Men, remembering the message he had sent with the Manling. "We wait," he said.

"I would not have waited," hissed Sskar, lashing his tail.
His sister Sskitter buffeted him on the nose. He cried out once and was still.

At the head of the Men was one Man in white armor with a red figure emblazoned on his white shield.

It was when he saw this that the Great-Grandfather sighed. "Ssgggi," he said.

"How can you tell?" asked the Great-Grandmother. "He is too big and too wide and too old for our Ssgggi. Our Ssgggi was this tall," and she drew a line into the pine tree that stood by the cave door.

"Men do not grow as dragons grow," reminded the Great-Grandfather gently. "They have no egg to protect their early days. Their skin is soft. They die young."

The Great-Grandmother put her paw on a certain spot on her nose and sighed. "It is not *our* Ssgggi," she said again. "He would not lead so many Men to our cave. He would not have to wear false scales on his body. He would come to the mountain by himself. I am going to scorch that counterfeit Ssgggi. I will roast him before his friends and crack his bones and suck out the marrow."

Then the Great-Grandfather of All Dragons knew that she spoke out of sorrow and anger and fear. He flicked a red tear from his own eye with his tail and held it to her. "See, my eyes cry for our grown-up and grown-away Manling," he said. "But though he is bigger and older, he is our Ssgggi nonetheless. I told him to identify himself when he returned so that we might know him. He has done so. What do you see on his shield?"

16

The Great-Grandmother rose to her feet and peered closely at the Man so many slithes below them. And those dragon eyes, which can see even the movement of a rabbit cowering in its burrow, saw the figure of a red dragon crouched on the white shield.

"I can see a mole in its den," said Sskar. "I can see a shrew in its tunnel. I can see . . ."

"You will see very little when I get finished with you if you do not shut up," said Sskitter and hit him once again.

"I see a red dragon," said the Great-Grandmother, her tail switching back and forth with anger.

"And what is the dragon doing?" asked the Great-Grandfather even more gently.

She looked again. Then she smiled, showing every one of her primary teeth. "It is covering a certain spot on its nose," she said.

7.

Just then the army stopped at a signal from the white knight. They dismounted from their horses and waited. The white knight raised his shield toward the mountain and shouted. It took a little while for his voice to reach the dragons, but when it did, they both smiled, for the white knight greeted them in the old tongue.

He said: "I send greetings. I am Ssgggi, the dragon who looks like a Man. I am taller now, but nowhere near as tall as a dragon. I am wiser now, but nowhere near as wise as a dragon. And I have brought a message from Men."

"Of course they did not trust him. Not a Man. Did they?" hissed Sskar.

"They trusted this Man," said Sskitter. "Oh, I know they did. I know I do."

Sskarma closed her eyes in thought. The other two little dragons were half asleep.

17

Grandfather Dragon did not answer their questions, but let the story answer the questions for him.

The Great-Grandfather of All Dragons stretched and rose. He unfurled his wings to their farthest point and opened his mouth and roared out gout after gout of flames. All the knights save the white knight knelt in fear. And then the Great-Grandfather pumped his wings twice and leaped into the air. Boulders buffeted by the winds rolled down the mountainside toward the Men.

The Great-Grandmother followed him, roaring as she flew. And they circled around and around in a great, widening gyre that was much too high for the puny Man arrows to reach.

Then the white knight called on all his archers to put down their bows, and the others to put aside their weapons. Reluctantly they obeyed, though a few grumbled angrily and they were all secretly very much afraid.

When the white knight saw that all his knights had disarmed themselves, he held his shield up once more and called out "Come, Worm" in his own tongue. He made the Man sign again, head to heart, shoulder to shoulder. At that signal, the Great-Grandfather of All Dragons and his mate came down. They crested a current of air and rode it down to the knight's feet.

When they landed, they jarred nearly fifty slithes of earth, causing several of the Men to fall over in amazement or fear or from the small quaking of the ground. Then the dragons lowered their heads to Ssgggi.

And the Man walked over to them, and first to the Great-Grandmother and then to the Great-Grandfather he lifted his fist and placed it ever so gently on a certain spot on the nose.

The Great-Grandmother thrummed at this. And then the Great-Grandfather thrummed as well. And the white knight joined them.

The two dragons' bodies shook loud and long with their thrumming. And the army of Men stared and then laughed and finally cheered, for they thought that the great-grandparents were afraid.

"Afraid? Afraid of puny Men? They were shaking because they were thrumming. Only lower *animals like rabbits and lion and deer—and Men—shake when they are afraid. I'll show them afraid!" cried Sskar. He leaped into the air and roared so hard that this time real flames came out of his nose slits, which so surprised him that he turned a flip in the air and came back to earth on his tailbone, which hurt enormously.*

Grandfather Dragon ignored him, and so did the other little dragons. Only Mother Dragon, from her corner in the cave, chuckled. It was a sound that broke boulders.

Sskar limped back proudly to his grandfather's side, eager to hear the rest of the story. "I showed them, didn't I?" he said.

8.

"Hear this," said the white knight Georgi, first in Man talk and then in the old tongue so that the dragons could understand as well. "From now on dragons shall raid no Man lands, and Men shall leave dragons alone. We will not even recognize you should we see you. You are no longer real to us.

"In turn, dragons will remain here, in this vast mountain wilderness untouched by Men. You will not see us or prey on us. You will not even recognize us. We are no longer real to dragons."

The Great-Grandfather roared out his agreement, as did the Great-Grandmother. Their roaring shattered a small mountain, which, to this day, Men called Dragon's Fall. Then they sprang up and were gone out of the sight of the army of Men, out of the lives of Men.

"Good," said Sskar. "I am glad they are out of our sight and out of our

lives. Men are ugly and unappetizing. We are much better off without them." He stretched and curled and tried to fall asleep. Stories made him feel uncomfortable and sleepy at the same time.

But Sskitter was not happy with the ending. "What of Ssgggi?" she said. "Did they ever see him again? Of all Men, he was my favorite."

"And what of the dragons' Thanksgiving?" said the littlest two, wide awake now.

Sskarma was silent, looking far out across the plains, across to Dragon's Fall, where the boulders lay all in a jumble.

Grandfather touched Sskarma's shoulder gently. "There is more," he said.

She turned her head to look at him, her black eyes glistening. "I know," she said. "Ssgggi came back. He would have to. He loved them so. And they loved him."

Grandfather shook his head. "No," he said. "He never came back. He could not. Dragons no longer existed for him, except in his heart. Did not exist for him—or for any Men. Of course," Grandfather added, "Men still exist for us. We do not have Man's gift of tongue or of the imagination. What is—for dragons—is. We cannot wish it away. We cannot make the real unreal, or the unreal real. I envy Man this other gift."

Sskarma closed her eyes and tried not to cry. "Never?" she asked softly. "He never came back? Then how could there have been a Thanksgiving?"

Dragons keep promises *Grandfather continued* for they do not have the imagination to lie. And so the Great-Grandfather and the Great-Grandmother and all their children, for they finally had many, and their children's children never bothered Men again. And, since Men did not believe dragons existed, Men did not bother dragons. That is what dragons give thanks for. In fact, Men believed that Saint George—as they called him in later years—had rid them forever of dragons.

And so things have stood to this very day.

9.

Mother Dragon rose at the story's end. "You have a Man's imagination, old one, though you deny it. You have a gift for making up stories, which is another way of saying you lie. Sometimes I think you are more Man than dragon."

"I tell the truth," growled the old dragon. "This is dragon history." Huffily, he cleaned his front claws.

"It is true that the word history contains the word story," said Mother Dragon. "But that is the only thing I will admit."

Grandfather Dragon houghed, and the smoke straggled out of his nose slits.

"And now if we are to have a real old-fashioned dragons' Thanksgiving, to celebrate the end of stories and the beginning of food, I will have to go hunting again," said Mother Dragon. "A deer, I think. I saw a fat herd by Dragon's Fall, grazing on the sweet spring grass."

"May I come?" asked Sskar.

Mother Dragon smiled and groomed his tail for him. "Now that you have real flames you may."

"The others and I will gather chestnuts," said Grandfather. "For the celebration. For Thanksgiving."

Sskarma shook her head. "I would like to stay behind and clean the cave."

The others left without an argument. No one liked to clean the cave, sweeping the bones over the side of the cliff. Mother Dragon and Sskar rose into the air, banked to the left, and winged out of sight so that they could approach the Fall from downwind. Grandfather Dragon and the three young dragons moved slowly along the deeply rutted mountain path.

Sskarma waited until they had all left; then she went out and looked at the great old pine tree that grew near the cave mouth. About five slithes up was a slash of white, the mark left by a dragon nail, a slash they all called Ssgggi's Mark. She looked at it for a long time and calculated how quickly trees grow. Then she stood up alongside the tree. The mark came up to her shoulder.

"Ssgggi," she said. Then she said it three more times. The fourth time she said it, it came out "Georgi."

21

"Georgi," she said a fifth time. This time it sounded right. Smiling quietly to herself, Sskarma glanced around the wilderness and then once into the sky. Far away she could see one of the great silver birds Grandfather always warned them about. "Georgi," she said, and went back in to clean the cave.

The Drabble Project was an idea begun by British writers Rob Meade and David Wake. They asked one hundred authors to each write a fantasy or science fiction story of exactly one hundred words. (The title doesn't count.) Profits from the book were donated to the Royal National Institute for the Blind's Talking Book project.

I was one of the authors asked to contribute to the second volume, and writing my story "The Dragon Woke and Stretched" was a pleasant—if exacting—diversion.

Then Ed Meskys, a blind American science fiction fan and publisher, took up a similar project. Only to make things even more difficult, he required a fifty-word story—fifty words, no more no less. (Title again doesn't count.)

The result this time was " 'Story,' the Old Man Said,". Curiously, both these minimalist stories of mine are about dragons.

The Dragon Woke and Stretched

Pulling thin lips over her teeth, she yawned heavily. It was winter and she was white again, the blood running thin through her leathery wings.

Behind her towered the black mountains; it had been a snowless year.

She shook herself, dislodging several branches from her nest, then leaped into the sky.

When they shot her the blood blossomed bright against her white breast. Falling to the ground, she shook the mountain, too large for them to cart away.

By morning, when they returned with knives, she was covered with nestlings lapping at her blood like human babes at the breast.

23

"Story," the Old Man Said,

looking beyond the cave to the dragon's tracks. "Story is our wall against the dark."

He told the tale: the landing, the first death, the second.

They heard the rush of wind, the terrible voice, a scream, then another.

Beyond the wall, the dragon waited but could not get in.

A friend of mine named Orson Scott Card was putting together Dragons of Light, *an anthology of stories about dragons, and asked me if I might have one to contribute.*

It so happened that I had been thinking about a story set on another planet in which dragons were set upon one another in great pits like fighting roosters (which is where the title comes from) or pit bulls. Pit bull fights and cockfights had been much in the news at the time; I thought them hideous sports.

So I wrote my story, which turned out to be only the beginning of my fascination with the dragon pits of Austar IV. I ended up writing an entire trilogy consisting of Dragon's Blood, Heart's Blood, *and* A Sending of Dragons. *I get letters from equally fascinated readers almost every week about the books. One time I showed up to speak at a school, and the entire sixth grade was dressed in costume, like Jakkin, with bond bags around their necks. Even the teachers!*

By the way, fewmets *is a real word. It comes from the medieval French word for spoor or dung. I first came upon it in T. H. White's brilliant books about King Arthur,* The Sword in the Stone *and its sequels.*

Cockfight

The pit cleaners circled noisily, gobbling up the old fewmets with their iron mouths. They spat out fresh sawdust and moved on. It generally took several minutes between fights, and the mechanical clanking of the cleaners was matched by the roars of the pit-wise dragons and the last-minute betting calls of their masters.

Jakkin heard the noises through the wooden ceiling as he groomed his dragon in the under-pit stalls. It was the first fight for both of them and Jakkin's fingers reflected his nervousness. He simply could not keep them still. They picked off bits of dust and flicked at specks on the dragon's already gleaming scales. They polished and smoothed and polished again. The red dragon seemed oblivious to first-fight jitters and arched up under Jakkin's hands.

Jakkin was pleased with his dragon's color. It was a dull red. Not the red of the hollyberry or the red of the wild flowering trillium, but the red of life's blood spilt upon the sand. It was a fighter's color, and he had known it from the first. That was why he had sneaked the dragon from its nest, away from its hatchlings, when the young worm had emerged from its egg in the sand of the nursery.

The dragon had looked then like any lizard, for it had not yet shed its eggskin, which was wrinkled and yellow, like custard scum. But Jakkin had sensed, beneath the skin, a darker shadow and had known it would turn red. Not many would have known, but Jakkin had, though he was only thirteen.

The dragon was not his, not really, for it had belonged to his master's nursery, just as Jakkin did. But on Austar IV there was only one way to escape from bond, and that was with gold. There was no quicker way to get gold than as bettor in the dragon pits. And there was nothing Jakkin wanted more than to be free. He had lived over half his life bonded to the nursery, from the time his parents had died when he was four. And most of that time he had worked as a stall boy, no better than a human pit cleaner, for Sarkkhan's Dragonry. What did it matter that he lived and slept and ate with his master's dragons? He was allowed to handle only their fewmets and spread fresh sawdust for their needs. If he could not raise a fighting dragon himself and buy his way out of bond, he would end up an *old* stall boy, like Likkarn, who smoked blisterweed, dreamed his days away, and cried red tears.

So Jakkin had watched and waited and learned as much as a junior stall boy could about dragon ways and dragon lore, for he knew the only way out of bond was to steal that first egg and raise it up for fighting or breeding or, if need was great, for the stews. But Jakkin did not know eggs, could sense nothing through the elastic shell, and so he had stolen a young dragon instead. It was a greater risk, for eggs were never counted but the new-hatched dragons were. At Sarkkhan's Dragonry old Likkarn kept the list of hatchlings. He was the only one of the bonders who could write, though Jakkin had taught himself to read a bit.

Jakkin had worried all through the first days that Likkarn would know and, knowing, tell. He kept the hatchling in a wood crate turned upside down way out in the sands. He swept away his footsteps to and from the crate and reckoned his way to it at night by the stars. And somehow he had not been found out. His reward had come as the young worm had grown.

First the hatchling had turned a dull brown and could trickle smoke through its nose slits. The wings on its back, crumpled and weak, had slowly stretched to a rubbery thickness. For days it had remained mud colored. Another boy might have sold it then to the stews, keeping the small fee in his leather bond bag that swung from the metal bond chain around his neck. It would have been a laughable amount, a coin or two at the most, and the bag would have looked just as empty as before.

But Jakkin had waited and the dragon finally molted, patchworking into a red. The nails on its foreclaws, which had been as brittle as jingle shells, were now as hard as golden oak and the same color. Its hindclaws were dull and strong as steel. Its eyes were two black shrouds and it had not roared yet, but Jakkin knew that roar would come, loud and full and fierce, when it was first blooded in the ring. The quality of the roar would start the betting rippling again through the crowd who judged a fighter by the timbre of its voice.

Jakkin could hear the cleaners clanking out of the ring through the mecho-holes. He ran his fingers through his straight brown hair and tried to swallow, then touched a dimple on his cheek that was as deep as a blood score. His hand found the bond bag and kneaded it several times for luck.

"Soon now," he promised the red dragon in a hoarse whisper, his hand still on the bag. "Soon. We will show them a first fight. They will remember us."

The red was too busy munching on burnwort to reply.

A disembodied voice announced the next fight. "Jakkin's Red, Mekkle's Bottle O' Rum."

Jakkin winced. He knew a little about Mekkle's dragon already. He had heard about it that morning as they had come into the pit stalls. Dragon masters and trainers did not chatter while they groomed their fighters, but bettors did, gathering around the favorites and trading stories of other fights. Mekkle's Rum was a light-colored male that favored its left side and had won three of its seven fights—the last three. It would never be great, the whispers had run, but it was good enough, and a hard draw for a new dragon, possibly disastrous for a would-be dragon master. Jakkin knew his red could be good with time, given the luck of the draw. It had all the things a dragon fighter was supposed to have: it had heart, it listened well, it did all he asked of it. But just as Jakkin had never run a fighter before, the red had never been in a ring. It had never been blooded or given roar. It did not even have its true name yet. Already, he knew, the betting was way against the young red and he could hear the murmur of new bets after the announcement. The odds would be so awful, he might never be able to get a sponsor for a second match. First fights were free, but seconds cost gold. And if he had no sponsor, that would leave only the stews for the dragon and a return to bond for himself.

Jakkin stroked the bond bag once more, then buttoned his shirt up to conceal it. He did not know yet what it felt like to be free, so he could stand more years as a bonder. And there might always be another chance to steal. But how could he ever give up the red to the stews? It was not any old dragon, it was his. They had already shared months of training, long nights together under the Austar moons. He knew its mind better than his own. It was a deep glowing cavern of colors and sights and sounds. He remembered the first time he had really felt his way into it, lying on his side, winded from running, the red beside him, a small mountain in the sand. The red calmed him when he was not calm, cheered him when he thought he could not be cheered. Linked as he was with it now, how could he bear to hear its last screams in the stews and stay sane? Perhaps that was why Likkarn was always yelling at the younger bonders, why he smoked blisterweed that turned the mind foggy and made a man cry red tears. And perhaps that was why dragons in the stews were always yearlings or the untrained. Not because they were softer, more succulent, but because no one would hear them when they screamed.

Jakkin's skin felt slimed with perspiration and the dragon sniffed it on him, giving out a few straggles of smoke from its slits. Jakkin fought down his own fear. If he could not control it, his red would have no chance at all, for a dragon was only as good as its master. He took deep breaths and then moved over to the red's head. He looked into its black, unblinking eyes.

"Thou art a fine one, my red," he whispered. "First fight for us both, but I trust thee." Jakkin always spoke *thou* to his dragon. He felt, somehow, it brought them closer. "Trust me?"

The dragon responded with slightly rounded smokes. Deep within its eyes Jakkin thought he detected small lights.

"Dragon's fire!" he breathed. "Thou *art* a fighter. I knew it!"

Jakkin slipped the ring from the red dragon's neck and rubbed its scales underneath. They were not yet as hard as a mature fighter's and for a moment he worried that the older Bottle O' Rum might tear the young dragon beyond repair. He pulled the red's head down and whispered into its ear. "Guard thyself here," he said, rubbing with his fingers under the tender neck links and thinking danger at it.

The dragon shook its head playfully and Jakkin slapped it lightly on the neck. With a surge, the red dragon moved out of the stall, over to the dragonlock, and flowed up into the ring.

"It's eager," the whisper ran around the crowd. They always liked that in young dragons. Time enough to grow cautious in the pit. Older dragons often were reluctant and had to be prodded with jumpsticks behind the wings or in the tender underparts of the tail. The bettors considered that a great fault. Jakkin heard the crowd's appreciation as he came up into the stands.

It would have been safer for Jakkin to remain below, guiding his red by mind. That way there would be no chance for Master Sarkkhan to find him here, though he doubted such a well-known breeder would enter a backcountry pit fight. And many trainers, Mekkle being one of them, stayed in the stalls drinking and smoking and guiding their dragons where the crowd could not influence them. But Jakkin needed to see the red as well as feel it, to watch the fight through his own eyes as well as the red's. They had trained too long at night, alone, in the sands. He did not know how another dragon in a real fight would respond. He had to see to understand it all. And the red was used to him being close by. He did not want to change that now. Besides, unlike many of the other bonders, he had never been to a fight, only read about them in books and heard about them from his bond mates. This might be his only chance. And, he further rationalized, up in the stands he might find out more about Mekkle's orange that would help him help the red.

Jakkin looked around the stands cautiously from the stairwell. He saw no one he knew, neither fellow bonders nor masters who had traded with Sarkkhan. He edged quietly into the stands, just one more boy at the fights. Nothing called attention to him but the empty bond bag beneath his shirt. He checked his buttons carefully to make sure they were closed. Then he leaned forward and watched as his red circled the ring.

It held its head high and measured the size of the pit, the height of the walls. It looked over the bettors as if it were counting them, and an appreciative chuckle went through the crowd. Then the red scratched in the sawdust several times, testing its depth. And still Bottle O' Rum had not appeared.

Then, with an explosion, Bottle O' Rum came through the dragon-lock and landed with all four feet planted well beneath the level of the sawdust, his claws fastened immovably to the boards.

"Good stance," shouted someone in the crowd and the betting began anew.

The red gave a little flutter with its wings, a flapping that might indicate nervousness, and Jakkin thought at it: "He is a naught. A stander. But thy nails and wings are fresh. Do not be afraid. Remember thy training." At that the little red's head went high and its neck scales glittered in the artificial sun of the pit.

"Watch that neck," shouted a heckler. "There's one that'll be blooded soon."

"Too soon," shouted another from across the stands at him.

Bottle O' Rum charged the inviting neck.

It was just as Jakkin hoped, for charging from the fighting stance is a clumsy maneuver at best. The claws must be retracted simultaneously, and the younger the dragon the more brittle its claws. The orange, Rum, was seven fights older than the red, but it was not yet mature. As Rum charged, one of the nails on his front right claw

32

caught in the floorboards and splintered, causing him to falter for a second. The red shifted its position slightly. Instead of blooding the red on the vulnerable neck, Rum's charge brought him headlong onto the younger dragon's chest plates, the hardest and slipperiest part of a fighting dragon's armor. The screech of teeth on scale brought winces from the crowd. Only Jakkin was ready, for it was a maneuver he had taught his dragon out in the hidden sands.

"Now!" he cried out and thought at once.

The young red needed no urging. It bent its neck around in a fast, vicious slash, and blood spurted from behind the ears of Mekkle's Rum.

"First blood!" cried the crowd.

Now the betting would change, Jakkin thought with a certain pleasure, and touched the bond bag through the thin cloth of his shirt. Ear bites bled profusely but were not important. It would hurt the orange dragon a little, like a pinprick or a splinter does a man. It would make the dragon mad and—more important—a bit more cautious. But first blood! It looked good.

Bottle O' Rum roared with the bite, loud and piercing. It was too high up in the throat yet with surprising strength. Jakkin listened carefully, trying to judge. He had heard dragons roar at the nursery in mock battles or when the keepers blooded them for customers intent on hearing the timbre before buying. To him the roar sounded as if it had all its power in the top tones and none that resonated. Perhaps he was wrong, but if his red could *outlast* the orange, it might impress this crowd.

In his eagerness to help his dragon, Jakkin moved to the pit rail. He elbowed his way through some older men.

"Here, youngster, what do you think you're doing?" A man in a gray leather coverall spoke. He was obviously familiar with the pits. Anyone in leather knew his way around. And his face, what

33

could be seen behind the gray beard, was scored with dragonblood scars.

"Get back up in the stands. Leave ringside to the money men," said his companion, taking in Jakkin's leather-patched cloth shirt and trousers with a dismissing look. He ostentatiously jounced a full bag that hung from his wrist on a leather thong.

Jakkin ignored them, fingering his badge with the facs picture of the red on it. He leaned over the rail. "Away, away, good red," he thought at his dragon and smiled when the red immediately wheeled and winged up from its blooded foe. Only then did he turn and address the two scowling bettors. "Pit right, good sirs," he said with deference, pointing at the same time to his badge.

They mumbled, but moved aside for him.

The orange dragon in the pit shook its head and the blood beaded its ears like a crown. A few drops spattered over the walls and into the stands. Each place a drop touched burned with that glow peculiar to the acidy dragon's blood. One watcher in the third row of the stands was not quick enough and was seared on the cheek. He reached up a hand to the wound but did not move from his place.

The orange Rum stood up tall again and dug back into the dust.

"Another stand," said the gray leather man to Jakkin's right.

"Pah, that's all it knows," said the dark man beside him. "That's how it won its three fights. Good stance, but that's it. I wonder why I bet it at all. Let's go and get something to smoke. This fight's a bore."

Jakkin watched them leave from the corner of his eye, but he absorbed their information. If the orange was a stander, if the information was true, it would help him with the fight.

The red dragon's leap back had taken it to the north side of the pit. When it saw that Bottle O' Rum had chosen to stand, it circled closer warily.

Jakkin thought at it, "He's good in the stance. Do not force him there. Make him come to thee."

The dragon's thoughts, as always, came back clearly to Jakkin wordless but full of color and emotion. The red wanted to charge; the dragon it had blooded was waiting. The overwhelming urge was to carry the fight to the foe.

"No, my red. Trust me. Be eager but not foolish," cautioned Jakkin, looking for an opening.

But the crowd, as eager as the young dragon, was communicating with it, too. The yells of the men, their thoughts of charging, over-powered Jakkin's single line of calm. The red started to move.

When it saw the red bunching for a charge, Rum solidified his stance. His shoulders went rigid with the strain. Jakkin knew that if his red dived at that standing rock, it could quite easily break a small bone in its neck. And rarely did a dragon come back to the pit once its neck bones had been set. Then it was good only for the breeding nurseries—if it had a fine pit record—or the stews.

"Steady, steady," Jakkin said, aloud. Then he shouted and waved a hand, "NO!"

The red had already started its dive, but the movement of Jakkin's hand was a signal too powerful for it to ignore, and at the last possible moment, it pulled to one side. As it passed, Rum slashed at it with a gaping mouth and shredded its wingtip.

"Blood," the crowd roared and waited for the red dragon to roar back.

Jakkin felt its confusion and his head swam with the red of dragon's blood as his dragon's thoughts came to him. He watched as it soared to the top of the building and scorched its wingtip on the artificial sun, cauterizing the wound. Then, still hovering, it opened its mouth for its first blooded roar.

There was no sound.

"A mute!" called a man from the stands. He spit angrily to one side. "Never heard one before."

A wit near him shouted back, "You won't hear this one, either."

The crowd laughed at this, and passed the quip around the stands.

But Jakkin only stared up at his red bitterly. "A mute," he thought at it. "You are as powerless as I."

His use of the distancing pronoun *you* further confused the young dragon, and it began to circle downward in a disconsolate spiral, closer and closer to the waiting Rum, its mind a maelstrom of blacks and grays.

Jakkin realized his mistake in time. "It does not matter," he cried out in his mind. "Even with no roar, thou wilt be great." He said it with more conviction than he really felt, but it was enough for the red. It broke out of its spiral and hovered, wings working evenly.

The maneuver, however, was so unexpected that the pit-wise Bottle O' Rum was bewildered. He came out of his stance with a splattering of dust and fewmets, stopped, then charged again. The red avoided him easily, landing on his back and raking the orange scales with its claws. That drew no blood, but it frightened the older dragon into a hindfoot rise. Balancing on his tail, Rum towered nearly eight feet high, his front claws scoring the air, a single shot of fire streaking from his slits.

The red backwinged away from the flames and waited.

"Steady, steady," thought Jakkin, in control again. He let his mind recall for them both the quiet sands and the cool nights when they had practiced with the wooden dragon-form on charges and clawing. Then Jakkin repeated out loud, "Steady, steady."

A hard hand on his shoulder broke through his thoughts and the sweet-strong smell of blisterweed assailed him. Jakkin turned.

37

"Not so steady yourself," came a familiar voice.

Jakkin stared up at the ravaged face, pocked with blood scores and stained with tear lines.

"Likkarn," breathed Jakkin, suddenly and terribly afraid.

Jakkin tried to turn back to the pit where his red waited. The hand on his shoulder was too firm, the fingers like claws through his shirt.

"And how did *you* become a dragon trainer?" the man asked.

Jakkin thought to bluff. The old stall boy was often too sunk in his smoked dreams to really listen. Bluff and run, for the wild anger that came after blister dreams never gave a smoker time to reason. "I found . . . found an egg, Likkarn," he said. And it could be true. There were a few wild dragons, bred from escapes that had gone feral.

The man said nothing but shook his head.

Jakkin stared at him. This was a new Likkarn, harder, full of purpose. Then Jakkin noticed. Lakkarn's eyes were clearer than he had ever seen them, no longer the furious pink of the weeder, but a softer rose. He had not smoked for several days at least. It was useless to bluff or run. "I took it from the nursery, Likkarn. I raised it in the sands. I trained it at night, by the moons."

"That's better. Much better. Liars are an abomination," the man said with a bitter laugh. "And you fed it what? Goods stolen from the Master, I wager. You born-bonders know nothing. Nothing."

Jakkin's cheeks were burning now. "I am no born-bonder. And I would never steal from the Master's stores. I planted in the sands last year and grew blisterweed and burnwort. I gathered the rest in the swamps. *On my own time.*" He added that fiercely.

"Bonders have no time of their own," Likkarn muttered savagely. "And supplements?"

"The Master says supplements are bad for a fighter. They make a fighter fast in the beginning, but they dilute the blood." Jakkin looked into Likkarn's eyes more boldly now. "I heard the Master say that. To a buyer."

Likkarn's smile was wry and twisted. "And you eavesdrop as well." He gave Jakkin's shoulder a particularly vicious wrench.

Jakkin gasped and closed his eyes with the pain. He wanted to cry out, and thought he had, when he realized it was not his own voice he heard but a scream from the pit. He pulled away from Likkarn and stared. The scream was Bottle O' Rum's, a triumphant roar as he stood over the red, whose injured wing was pinioned beneath Rum's right front claw.

"*Jakkin . . .*" came Likkarn's voice behind him, full of warning. How often Jakkin had heard that tone right before old Likkarn had roused from a weed dream to the fury that always followed. Likkarn was old, but his fist was still solid.

Jakkin trembled, but he willed his focus onto the red, whose thoughts came tumbling back into his head now in a tangle of muted colors and whines. He touched his hand to the small lump under his shirt where the bond bag hung. He could feel his own heart beating through the leather shield. "Never mind, my red," soothed Jakkin. "Never mind the pain. Recall the time I stood upon thy wing and we played at the Great Upset. Recall it well, thou mighty fighter. Remember. Remember."

The red stirred only slightly and made a flutter with its free wing. The crowd saw this as a gesture of submission. So did Rum and, through him, his master, Mekkle. But Jakkin did not. He knew the red had listened well and understood. The game was not over yet. Pit fighting was not all brawn; how often Master Sarkkhan had said that. The best fighters, the ones who lasted for years, were cunning gamesters and it was this he had guessed about his red from the first.

The fluttering of the unpinioned wing caught Bottle O' Rum's eye

39

and the orange dragon turned toward it, relaxing his hold by a single nail.

The red fluttered its free wing again. Flutter and feint. Flutter and feint. It needed the orange's attention totally on that wing. Then its tail could do the silent stalking it had learned in the sands with Jakkin.

Bottle O' Rum followed the fluttering as though laughing for his own coming triumph. His dragon jaws opened slightly in a deadly grin. If Mekkle had been in the stands instead of below in the stalls, the trick might not have worked. But the orange dragon, intent on the fluttering wing, leaned his head way back and fully opened his jaws, readying for the kill. He was unaware of what was going on behind him.

"Now!" shouted Jakkin in his mind and only later realized that the entire stands had roared the words with him. Only the crowd had been roaring for the wrong dragon.

The red's tail came around with a snap, as vicious and as accurate as a driver's whip. It caught the orange on its injured ear and across an eye.

Rum screamed instead of roaring and let go of the red's wing. The red was up in an instant and leaped for Bottle O' Rum's throat.

One, two, and the ritual slashes were made. The orange throat was coruscated with blood and Rum instantly dropped to the ground.

Jakkin's dragon backed at once, slightly akilter because of the wound in its wing.

"Game to Jakkin's Red," said the disembodied voice over the speaker.

The crowd was strangely silent. Then a loud whoop sounded from one voice buried in the stands, a bettor who had taken a chance on the First Fighter.

That single voice seemed to rouse Bottle O' Rum. He raised his head from the ground groggily. Only his head and half his neck cleared the dust. He strained to arch his neck over, exposing the underside to the light. The two red slashes glistened like thin hungry mouths. Then Rum began a strange, horrible humming that changed to a high-pitched whine. His body began to shake and the shaking became part of the sound as the dust eddied around him.

The red dragon swooped down and stood before the fallen Rum, as still as stone. Then it, too, began to shake.

The sound changed from a whine to a high roar. Jakkin had never heard anything like it before. He put his hands to the bond bag, then to his ears.

"What is it? What is happening?" he cried out, but the men on either side of him had moved away. Palms to ears, they backed toward the exits. Many in the crowd had already gone down the stairs, setting the thick wood walls between themselves and the noise.

Jakkin tried to reach the red dragon's mind, but all he felt were storms of orange winds, hot and blinding, and a shaft of burning white light. As he watched, the red rose up on its hind legs and raked the air frantically with its claws as if getting ready for some last deadly blow.

"Fool's Pride," came Likkarn's defeated voice behind him, close enough to his ear to hear. "That damnable dragon wants death. He has been shamed and he'll scream your red into it. Then you'll know. All you'll have left is a killer on your hands. I lost three that way. *Three.* Fool's Pride." He shouted the last at Jakkin's back, for at his first words, Jakkin had thrown himself over the railing into the pit. He landed on all fours, but was up and running at once.

He had heard of Fool's Pride, that part of the fighting dragon's bloody past that was not always bred out. Fool's Pride that led some defeated dragons to demand death. It had nearly caused dragons to become extinct. If men had not carefully watched the lines, trained the fighters to lose with grace, there would have been no dragons left on Austar IV. A good fighter should have a love of blooding, yes. But killing made dragons unmanageable, made them feral, made them wild.

Jakkin crashed into the red's side. "No, no," he screamed up at it, beating on its body with his fists. "Do not wet thy jaws in his death." He reached as high as he could and held on to the red's neck. The scales slashed one of his palms, but he did not let go.

It was his touch more than his voice or his thoughts that stopped the young red. It turned slowly, sluggishly, as if rousing from a dream. Jakkin fell from its neck to the ground.

The movement away shattered Bottle O' Rum's concentration. He slipped from screaming to unconsciousness in an instant.

The red nuzzled Jakkin, its eyes unfathomable, its mind still clouded. The boy stood up. Without bothering to brush the dust from his clothes, he thought at it, *"Thou mighty First."*

The red suddenly crowded his mind with victorious sunbursts, turned, then streaked back through the hole to its stall and the waiting burnwort.

Mekkle and two friends came up the stairs, glowering, leaped into the pit, and dragged the fainting orange out through a mecho-hole by his tail.

Only then did Jakkin walk back to ringside, holding his cut hand palm up. It had just begun to sting.

Likkarn, still standing by the railing, was already smoking a short strand of blisterweed. He stared blankly as the red smoke circled his head.

"I owe you," Jakkin said slowly up to him, hating to admit it. "I did not know Fool's Pride when I saw it. Another minute and the red would have been good for nothing but the stews. If I ever get a Second Fight, I will give you some of the gold. *Your bag is not yet full.*"

Jakkin meant the last phrase simply as ritual, but Likkarn's eyes suddenly roused to weed fury. His hand went to his throat. "You owe me nothing," said the old man. He held his head high and the age lines on his neck crisscrossed like old fight scars. "*Nothing.* You owe the Master everything. I need no reminder that I am a bonder. *I fill my bag myself.*"

Jakkin bowed his head under the old man's assault. "Let me tend the red's wounds. Then do with me as you will." He turned, and without waiting for an answer, ducked through the mecho-hole and slid down the shaft.

Jakkin came to the stall where the red was already at work grooming itself, polishing its scales with a combination of fire and spit. He slipped the ring around its neck and knelt down by its side. Briskly he put his hand out to touch its wounded wing, in a hurry to finish the examination before Likkarn came down. The red drew back at his touch, sending a mauve landscape into his mind, dripping with gray tears.

"Hush, little flametongue," crooned Jakkin, slowing himself down and using the lullaby sounds he had invented to soothe the hatchling of the sands. "I won't hurt thee. I want to help."

But the red continued to retreat from him, crouching against the wall.

Puzzled, Jakkin pulled his hand back, yet still the red huddled away, and a spurt of yellow-red fire flamed from its slits. "Not here, furnace-lung," said Jakkin, annoyed. "That will set the stall on fire."

A rough hand pushed him aside. It was Likkarn, no longer in the weed dream but starting into the uncontrollable fury that capped a weed sequence. The dragon, its mind open with the pain of its wound and the finish of the fight, had picked up Likkarn's growing anger and reacted to it.

"You don't know wounds," growled Likkarn. "I'll show you what

43

a *real* trainer knows." He grabbed the dragon's torn wing and held it firmly, then with a quick motion, and before Jakkin could stop him, he set his mouth on the jagged tear.

The dragon reared back in alarm and tried to whip its tail around, but the stalls were purposely built small to curb such motion. Its tail scraped along the wall and barely tapped the man. But Jakkin grabbed at Likkarn's arm with both hands and furiously tore him from the red's wing.

"I'll kill you, you weeder," he screamed. "Can't you wait till a dragon is in the stews before you try to eat it? I'll kill you." He slammed at Likkarn with his fist and feet, knowing as he did it that the man's weed anger would be turned on him and he might be killed by it, and not caring. Suddenly Jakkin felt himself being lifted up from behind, his legs dangling, kicking uselessly at the air. A strong arm around his waist held him fast. Another pushed Likkarn back against the wall.

"Hold off, boy. He was a good trainer—once. And he's right about the best way to deal with a wing wound. An open part, filled with dragon's blood, might burn the tongue surely. But a man's tongue heals quickly, and there is something in human saliva that closes these small tears."

Jakkin twisted around as best he could and saw the man he had most feared seeing. It was Master Sarkkhan himself, in a leather suit of the red-and-gold nursery colors. His red beard was brushed out and he looked grim.

Sarkkhan put the boy down but held on to him with one hand. With the other, he smoothed his hair back from a forehead that was pitted with blood scores as evenly spaced as a bonder's chain. "Now promise me you will let Likkarn look to the red's wing."

"I will not. He's a weeder and he's as likely to rip the red as heal

44

it and the red hates him—just as I do," shouted Jakkin. There he stopped and put the back of his hand over his mouth, shocked at his own bold words.

Likkarn raised his hand to the boy and aimed a blow at his head, but before the slap landed, the dragon nosed forward and pushed the man to the ground.

Master Sarkkhan let go of Jakkin's shoulder and considered the red for a moment. "I think the boy is right, Likkarn. The dragon won't have you. It's too closely linked. I wouldn't have guessed that, but there it is. Best leave this to the boy and me."

Likkarn got up clumsily and brushed off his clothes. His bond bag had fallen over the top of his overall bib in the scuffle and Jakkin was shocked to see that it was halfway plump, jangling with coins. Likkarn caught his look and angrily stuffed the bag back inside, then jabbed at the outline of Jakkin's bag under·his shirt with a reddened finger. "And how much have *you* got there, boy?" He walked off with as much dignity as he could muster to slump by the stairwell and watch.

Sarkkhan ignored them both and crouched down by the dragon, letting it get the smell of him. He caressed its jaws and under its neck with his large, scarred hands. Slowly the big man worked his way back toward the wings, crooning at the dragon in low tones, smoothing its scales, all the while staring into its eyes. Slowly the membranes, top and bottom, shuttered the red's eyes and it relaxed. Only then did Sarkkhan let his hand close over the wounded wing. The dragon gave a small shudder but was otherwise quite still.

"Your red did a good job searing its wound on the light. Did you teach it that?"

"No," the boy admitted.

"Of course not, foolish of me. How could you? No light in the

45

sands. Good breeding then," said Sarkkhan with a small chuckle of appreciation. "And I should know. After all, your dragon's mother is my best—Heart O' Mine."

"You . . . you knew all along, then." Jakkin felt as confused as a blooded First.

Sarkkhan stood up and stretched. In the confines of the stall he seemed enormous, a red-gold giant. Jakkin suddenly felt smaller than his years.

"*Fewmets*, boy, of course I knew," Sarkkhan answered. "I know *everything* that happens at my nursery."

Jakkin collapsed down next to his dragon and put his arm over its neck. When he finally spoke, it was in a very small voice. "Then why did you let me do it? Why did you let me steal the dragon? Were you trying to get me in trouble? Do you want me in jail?"

The man threw back his head and roared, and the dragons in neighboring stalls stirred uneasily at the sound. Even Likkarn started at the laugh and a trainer six stalls down growled in disapproval. Then Sarkkhan looked down at the boy, crouched by the red dragon. "I'm sorry, boy, I forget how young you are. Never known anyone quite that young to successfully train a hatchling. But every man gets a chance to steal one egg. It's a kind of test, you might say. The only way to break out of bond. Some men are meant to be bonders, some masters. How else can you tell? Likkarn's tried it—endless times, eh, old man?" The master glanced over at Likkarn with a look akin to affection, but Likkarn only glared back. "Steal an egg and try. The only things it is wrong to steal are a bad egg or your master's provisions." Sarkkhan stopped talking for a minute and mused, idly running a hand over the red dragon's back as it chewed contentedly now on its burnwort, little gray straggles of smoke easing from its slits. "Of course most *do* steal bad eggs or are too impatient to train what comes out and instead they make a quick sale to the stews just for a few coins to jangle in their bags. Then it's back to bond again before a month is out. It's only the ones who steal provisions that land in jail, boy."

"Then you won't put me in jail? Or the red in the stews? I couldn't let you do that, Master Sarkkhan. Not even you. I wouldn't let you. I . . ." Jakkin began to stutter as he often did in his master's presence.

"Send a First Fighter, a *winner* to the stews? *Fewmets*, boy, where's your brain? Been smoking blisterweed?" Sarkkhan hunkered down next to him.

Jakkin looked down at his sandals. His feet were soiled from the dust of the stall. He ordered his stomach to calm down, and he felt an answering muted rainbow of calm from the dragon. Then a peculiar thought came to him. "Did *you* have to steal an egg, Master Sarkkhan?"

The big redheaded man laughed and thrust his hand right into Jakkin's face. Jakkin drew back but Sarkkhan was holding up two fingers and wiggling them before his eyes.

"Two! I stole two. A male and a female. And it was not mere chance. Even then I knew the difference. *In the egg* I knew. And that's why I'm the best breeder on Austar IV." He stood up abruptly and held out his hand to the boy. "But enough. The red is fine and you are due upstairs." He yanked Jakkin to his feet and seemed at once to lose his friendliness.

"Upstairs?" Jakkin could not think what that meant. "You said I was not to go to jail. I want to stay with the red. I want . . ."

"*Worm-wort*, boy, have you been listening or not? You have to register that dragon, give her a name, record her as a First Fighter, a winner."

"*Her?*" Jakkin heard only the one word.

"Yes, a her. Do you challenge *me* on that? And I want to come with you and collect my gold. I bet a bagful on that red of yours— on Likkarn's advice. He's been watching you train, my orders. He

47

said she was looking good and sometimes I believe him." Sarkkhan moved toward the stairwell where Likkarn still waited. "I owe him, you know. He taught me everything."

"Likkarn? Taught you?"

They stopped by the old man who was slumped again in another blisterweed dream. Sarkkhan reached out and took the stringy red weed ash from the old man's hand. He threw it on the floor and ground it savagely into the dust. "He wasn't born a weeder, boy. And he hasn't forgotten all he once knew." Then, shaking his head, Master Sarkkhan moved up the stairs, impatiently waving a hand at the boy to follow.

A stray strand of color pearls passed through Jakkin's mind and he turned around to look at the dragon's stall. Then he gulped and said in a rush at Sarkkhan's back, "But she's a mute, Master. She may have won this fight by wiles, but she's a mute. No one will bet on a dragon that cannot roar."

The man reached down and grabbed Jakkin's hand, yanking him through the doorway and up the stairs. They mounted two at a time. "You really are lizard waste," said Sarkkhan, punctuating his sentences with another step. "Why do you think I sent a half-blind weeder skulking around the sands at night watching you train a snatchling? Because I'd lost my mind? *Fewmets*, boy. I want to know what is happening to every damned dragon I have bred because I have had a hunch and a hope these past two years, breeding small-voiced dragons together. I've been *trying* to breed a mute. Think of it, a mute fighter—why, it would give nothing away, not to pit foes or to the bettors. A mute fighter and its trainer . . ." Sarkkhan stopped on the stairs, looking down at the boy. "Why, they'd rule the pits, boy."

They finished the stairs and turned down the hallway. Sarkkhan strode ahead and Jakkin had to double-time in order to keep up with the big man's strides.

"Master Sarkkhan," he began at the man's back.

Sarkkhan did not break stride but growled, "I am no longer your master, Jakkin. *You* are a master now. A master trainer. That dragon will speak only to you, go only on your command. Remember that and act accordingly."

Jakkin blinked twice and touched his chest. "But . . . but my bag is empty. I have no gold to fill it. I have no sponsor for my next fight. I . . ."

Sarkkhan whirled, and his eyes were fierce. "*I* am sponsor for your next fight. I thought that much, at least, was clear. And when your bag is full, you will pay me no gold for your bond. Instead I want pick of the first hatching when the red is bred—to a mate of my choosing. If she is a complete mute, she may breed true, and *I* mean to have it."

"Oh, Master Sarkkhan," Jakkin cried, suddenly realizing that all his dreams were realities, "you may have the pick of the first *three* hatchings." He grabbed the man's hand and tried to shake his thanks into it.

"*Fewmets!*" the man yelled, startling some of the passersby. He shook the boy's hand loose. "How can you ever become a bettor if you offer it all up front? You have to disguise your feelings better than that. Offer me the pick of the *third* hatching. Counter me. Make me work for whatever I get."

Jakkin said softly, testing, "The pick of the third."

"First two," said Sarkkhan softly back and his smile came slowly. Then he roared, "Or I'll have you in jail and the red in the stews."

A crowd began to gather around them, betting on the outcome of the uneven match. Sarkkhan was a popular figure at pit fights and the boy was leather patched, obviously a bonder, an unknown, worm waste.

All at once Jakkin felt as if he were at pitside. He felt the red's mind flooding into his, a rainbow effect that gave him a rush of courage. It was a game, then, all a game. And he knew how to play. "The second," said Jakkin, smiling back. "After all, Heart's Blood is a First Fighter, and a winner. And"—he hissed at Sarkkhan so that only the two of them could hear—"she's a mute." Then he stood straight and said loudly so that it carried to the crowd. "You'll be lucky to have pick of the second."

Sarkkhan stood silently as if considering both the boy and the crowd. He brushed his hair back from his forehead, then nodded. "Done," he said. "A hard bargain." Then he reached over and ruffled Jakkin's hair and they walked off together.

The crowd, settling their bets, let them through.

"I *thought* you were a good learner," Sarkkhan said to the boy. "Second it is. Though," and he chuckled and said quietly, "you should remember this. There is never anything good in a first hatching. Second is the best by far."

"I didn't know," said Jakkin.

"Why should you?" countered Sarkkhan. "*You* are not the best breeder on Austar IV. I am. But I like the name you picked. Heart's Blood out of Heart O' Mine. It suits."

They went through the doorway together to register the red and to stuff Jakkin's bag with hard-earned dragon's gold.

I wrote a series of lullaby poems for a poetry collection, using mermaids and trolls as well as such real-life animals as owls and wolves and cats and bears. This was the title poem for the collection. Later I used a variant of the poem in my novel Dragon's Blood *and another in the story "Great-Grandfather Dragon's Tale." Once I get an idea I like, I hate to let it go. I call it recycling.*

Dragon Night

Little flame mouths,
Cool your tongues.
Dreamtime starts,
My furnace-lungs.

Rest your wings now,
Little flappers,
Cave mouth calls
To dragon nappers.

Night is coming,
Bank your fire.
Time for dragons
To retire.

Hiss.
Hush.
Sleep.

Heroes have always puzzled me. They never seem to know fear. Yet I have been in some terrifying situations (falling into the Colorado River while white-water rafting; being confronted by a bear in a spring meadow; finding one of my sons bleeding and dazed and unable to speak except in three questions, which he repeated endlessly for twenty-four hours), and I have acted quickly and decisively—and fallen apart afterward. Heroes never seem to fall apart—either before or after.

So I wanted to write a story in which the hero knows himself not to be a hero, and the audience knows him not to be a hero, and yet he is a hero despite it all.

Also I wanted to use the vast amount of kite-knowledge floating about in my brain. My father had been the International Kite Flying Champion and listed in the Guinness Book of World Records for keeping a kite aloft for seven days and one hour. I had written a big book about kites—World on a String. I know kites.

So I had a lot of links, but no story, until I found Lancot. (Yes, his name is supposed to remind you of Lancelot.) And once I let him meet the healer's three daughters, Tansy, Sage, and Rosemary (all plants of healing), the story moved along on its own.

People say imitation is the sincerest sort of flattery. Sometimes I imitate myself. There are lines in this story that are almost identical with lines in my other dragon stories. Does this mean I am flattering myself?

Though I made up most of the rhyming curses and spells, the one that begins "Fire and water on thy wing . . ." is a really old one I found somewhere, and it was absolutely appropriate. So I appropriated it. And the inscription on Great Tom is left over from research I did years ago when I wrote Ring Out: A Book of Bells. Drache is the German word that means both "dragon" and "kite." But "dragonsbane" is a plant I made up. I did. I did. At least I think I did!

Dragonfield

There is a spit of land near the farthest shores of the farthest islands. It is known as Dragonfield. Once dragons dwelt on the isles in great herds, feeding on the dry brush and fueling their flames with the carcasses of small animals and migratory birds. There are no dragons there now, though the nearer islands are scored with long furrows as though giant claws had been at work, and the land is fertile from the bones of the buried behemoths. Yet though the last of the great worms perished long before living memory, there is a tale still told by the farmers and fisherfolk of the isles about that last dragon.

His name in the old tongue was Aredd and his color a dull red. It was not the red of hollyberry or the red of the wild flowering trillium, but the red of a man's lifeblood spilled out upon the sand. Aredd's tail was long and sinewy, his body longer still. Great mountains rose upon his back. His eyes were black, and when he was angry, looked as empty as the eyes of a shroud, but when he was calculating, they shone with a false jeweled light. His jaws were a furnace that could roast a whole bull. And when he roared, he could be heard like distant thunder throughout the archipelago.

Aredd was the last of his kind and untaught in the riddle lore of dragons. He was but fierceness and fire, for he had hatched late from the brood. His brothers and sisters were all gone, slain in the famous Dragon Wars when even young dragons were spitted by warriors who had gone past fearing. But the egg that had housed Aredd had lain buried in the sand of Dragonfield years past the carnage, uncovered at last by an unnaturally high tide. And when he hatched, no one had remarked it. So the young worm had stretched and cracked the shell and emerged nose-first in the sand.

At the beginning he looked like any large lizard, for he had not yet shed his eggskin, which was lumpy and whitish, like clotted cream. But he grew fast, as dragons will, and before the week was out he was the size of a small pony and his eggskin had sloughed off. He had, of course, singed and eaten the skin and so developed a taste for crackling. A small black-snouted island pig was his next meal, then a family of shagged cormorants flying island-to-island on their long migration south.

And still no one remarked him, for it was the time of great harvests brought about by the fertilization of the rich high tides, and everyone was needed in the fields: old men and women, mothers with their babes tied to their backs, ardent lovers who might have slipped off to the far isle to tryst. Even the young fishermen did not dare to go down to the bay and cast off while daylight bathed the plants and vines. They gave up their nets and lines for a full two weeks to help with the "stripping," as the harvest was called then. And by night, of course, the villagers were much too weary to sail by moonlight to the spit.

Another week, then, and Aredd was a dull red and could trickle smoke rings through his nostrils, and he was the size of a bull. His wings, still crumpled and weak, lay untested along his sides, but his foreclaws, which had been as brittle as shells at birth, were now as hard as golden oak. He had sharpened them against the beach boulders, leaving scratches as deep as worm runnels. At night he dreamed of blood.

The tale of Aredd's end, as it is told in the farthest islands, is also the tale of a maiden who was once called Tansy after the herb of healing but was later known as Areddiana, daughter of the dragon. Of course it is a tale with a hero. That is why there are dragons, after all: to call forth heroes. But he was a hero in spite of himself and because of Tansy. The story goes thus:

There were three daughters of a healer who lived on the northern shore of Medd, the largest isle of the archipelago. Although they had proper names, after the older gods, they were always called by their herbal names.

Rosemary, the eldest, was a weaver. Her face was plain but honest looking, a face that would wear well with time. Her skin was dark as if she spent her days out in the sun, though, in truth, she preferred the cottage's cold dirt floors and warm hearth. Her lips were full but she kept them thin. She buffed the calluses on her hands to make them shine. She had her mother's gray eyes and her passion for work, and it annoyed her that others had not.

Sage was the beauty, but slightly simple. She was as golden as Rosemary was brown, and brushed her light-filled hair a full hundred strokes daily. When told to she worked, but otherwise preferred to stare out the window at the sea. She was waiting, she said, for her own true love. She had even put it in rhyme.

Glorious, glorious, over the sea,
My own true love will come for me.

She repeated it so often they all believed it to be true.

Tansy was no special color at all; rather she seemed to blend in with her surroundings, sparkling by a stream, golden in the sunny meadows, mouse-brown within the house. She was the one who was a trouble to her mother: early walking and always picking apart things that had been knit up with great care just to see what made them work. So she was named after the herb that helped women in their times of trouble. Tansy. It was hoped that she would grow into her name.

"Where *is* that girl?" May-Ma cried.

Her husband, crushing leaves for a poultice, knew without asking which girl she meant. Only with Tansy did May-Ma's voice take on an accusatory tone.

"I haven't seen her for several hours, May-Ma," said Rosemary from the loom corner. She did not even look up but concentrated on the marketcloth she was weaving.

"That Tansy. She is late again for her chores. Probably dreaming somewhere. Or eating some new and strange concoction." May-Ma's

55

hands moved on the bread dough as if preparing to beat a recalcitrant child. "Someday, mind you, someday she will eat herself past your help, Da."

The man smiled to himself. Never would he let such a thing happen to his Tansy. She had knowledge, precious, god-given, and nothing she made was past his talents for healing. Besides, she seemed to know instinctively how far to taste, how far to test, and she had a high tolerance for pain.

"Mind you," May-Ma went on, pounding the dough into submission, "now, mind you, I'm not saying she doesn't have a gift. But gift or no, she has chores to do." Her endless repetitions had begun with the birth of her first child and had increased with each addition to the family until now, three live children later (she never mentioned the three little boys buried under rough stones at the edge of the garden), she repeated herself endlessly. "Mind you, a gift is no excuse."

"I'm minding, May-Ma," said her husband, wiping his hands on his apron. He kissed her tenderly on the head as if to stanch the flow of words, but still they bled out.

"If she would remember her chores as well as she remembers dreams," May-Ma went on, "as well as she remembers the seven herbs of binding, the three parts to setting a broken limb, the . . ."

"I'm going, May-Ma," whispered her husband into the flood and left.

He went outside and down a gentle path that wound toward the river, guessing that on such a day Tansy would be picking cress.

The last turn opened onto the river and never failed to surprise him with joy. The river was an old one, its bends broad as it flooded into the great sea. Here and there the water had cut through soft rock to make islets that could be reached by poleboat or, in the winter, by walking across the thick ice. This turning, green down to the river's edge, was full of cress and reeds and even wild rice carried from the eastern lands by migrating birds.

"Tansy," he called softly, warning her of his coming.

A gull screamed back at him. He dropped his eyes to the hatch-marked tracks of shore birds in the mud, waited a moment to give her time to answer, and then when none came, called again. "Tansy. Child."

"Da, Da, here!" It was the voice of a young woman, breathless yet throaty, that called back. "And see what I have found. I do not know what it is."

The reeds parted and she stepped onto the grass. Her skirts were kilted up, bunched at her waist. Even so they were damp and muddy. Her slim legs were coated with a green slime and there was a smear of that same muck along her nose and across her brow where she had obviously wiped away sweat or a troublesome insect. She held up a sheaf of red grassy weeds, the tops tipped with pink florets. Heedless of the blisters on her fingers, she gripped the stalk.

"What is it?" she asked. "It hurts something fierce, but I've never seen it before. I thought you might know."

"Drop it. Drop it at once, child. Where are your mitts?"

At his cry, she let the stalk go and it landed in the water, spinning around and around in a small eddy, a spiral of smoke uncurling from the blossoms.

He plucked her hand toward him and reached into his belt bag. Taking out a cloth-wrapped packet of fresh aloe leaves, he broke one leaf in two and squeezed out the healing oils onto her hands. Soon the redness around the blisters on her fingers was gone, though the blisters remained like a chain of tiny seed pearls.

"Now will you tell me what it is?" she asked, grinning up at him despite what he knew to be a terribly painful burn. There was a bit of mischief in her smile, too, which kept him from scolding her further about her gloves.

"I have never seen it before, only heard of it. I thought it but a tale. It is called fireweed or flamewort. You can guess why. The little blisters on the hand are in the old rhyme. It grows only where a great dragon lives, or so the spellbook says:

Leaves of blood and sores of pearl,
In the sea, a smoky swirl,
Use it for your greatest need,
Dragon's bane and fireweed.

"They used it somehow in the Dragon Wars. But child, look at your hands!"

She looked down for the first time and caught her breath as she saw the tiny, pearly sores. "One, two, three . . . why, there must be fifteen blisters here," she said, fascinated. "Sores of pearl indeed. But what is its use?"

Her father shook his head and wrapped the aloe carefully. "I cannot imagine, since the sting of it is so fierce. And if the note about it be true, it will burn for near an hour once the florets open, burn with a hot steady flame that cannot be put out. Then it will crumble all at once into red ash. So you leave it there, steaming, on the water and come home with me. There is *no use* for dragon's bane, for there are no more dragons."

The fireweed had already lost its color in the river, graying out, but still it sent up a curl of blue-white steam. Tansy found a stick and pushed it toward the stalk and where she touched, the weed flared up again a bright red. When she pulled back the stick, the color of the weed faded as quickly as a blush. The stick burned down

58

toward Tansy's fingers and she dropped it into the river, where it turned to ash and floated away.

"Dragon's bane," she whispered. "And I wonder why." She neglected to mention to her father that there was a large patch of the weed growing hidden in the reeds.

"Such questions will not win you favor at home," her father said, taking her unblistered hand in his. "Especially not with your dear May-Ma ready to do your chores. She will chide you a dozen times over for the same thing if we do not hurry home."

"My chores!" Tansy cried. Then she shrugged and looked at her father with wise eyes. "Even if I were home to do them, I would hear of it again and again. Poor May-Ma, she speaks to herself for none of the rest of us really talks to her." She pulled away from him and was gone up the path as if arrowshot.

He chuckled aloud and walked to the water's edge to pick some fresh peppermint and sweet woodruff for teas. The river's slow meandering was still noisy enough that he did not hear the strange chuffing sound of heavy new wings above him. It was only when the swollen shadow darkened the ground that he looked up and into the belly of a beast he had thought long extinct. He was so surprised, he did not have time to cry out or to bless himself before dying. The flames that killed him were neither long nor especially hot, but fear and loathing added their toll. The healer was dead before his body touched earth. He never felt the stab of the golden claws as the dragon carried him back to its home on the far spit of land.

Only the singed open herb bag, its contents scattered on the path, bore testimony to the event.

They did not look for him until near dark. And then, in the dark, with only their small tapers for light, they missed the burned herb

59

sack. It was morning before they found it and Sage had run off to their closest neighbors for help.

What help could be given? The healer was gone, snatched from the good earth he had so long tended. They could not explain the singed sack, and so did not try. They concentrated instead on his missing body. Perhaps he had fallen, one man suggested, into the river. Since he was not a fisherman, he could not swim. They expected his body to fetch up against an island shore within a few days. Such a thing had happened to men before. The fisherfolk knew where to look. And that was all the comfort the villagers had to lend. It was harvest, after all, and they could spare only the oldest women to weep and prepare funeral pies.

"And what kind of funeral is it?" May-Ma asked repeatedly. "Without a body, what kind of burial? He will be back. Back to laugh at our preparations. I know it. I know it here." She touched her breast and looked out to the garden's edge and the large, newly cut stone overshadowing the three smaller ones. "He will be back."

But she was the only one to hold out such hope, and to no one's surprise but May-Ma's, the healer did not return. The priest marked his passing with the appropriate signs and psalms, then returned to help with the harvest. The girls wept quietly: Rosemary by her loom, dampening the cloth; Sage by the window, gazing off down the path; Tansy alone in the woods. May-Ma sobbed her hopes noisily and the villagers, as befitting their long friendship with the healer, spoke of his gift with reverence. It did not bring him back.

The healer's disappearance became a small mystery in a land used to small mysteries until after the harvest was in. And then Tam the carpenter's finest draft horse was stolen. A week and a half later, two prize ewes were taken from Mother Comfy's fold. And almost two weeks after that, the latest of the cooper's twelve children disappeared from its cradle in the meadow when the others had left it for just a moment to go and pick wild trillium in the dell. A great fear descended upon the village then. They spoke of ravening beasts, of blood-crazed goblins, of a mad changeling beast-man roaming the woods, and looked at one another with suspicion. The priest ranted of retribution and world's end. But none of them considered dragons, for as they knew full well, the last of the great worms had been killed in the Dragon Wars. And while none had actually seen a goblin or a beast-man, and while there had not been wild animals larger than a goldskin fox in the woods for twice two hundred years, still such creatures seemed likelier than dragons. Dragons, they knew with absolute and necessary conviction, were no more.

It was a fisherman who saw Aredd and lived to tell of it. In a passion one early morning he had gone over the side of his boat to untangle a line. It was a fine line, spun out over the long winter by his wife, and he was not about to lose it, for the mark of its spinning was still on his wife's forefinger and thumb. The line was down a great ways underwater and he had scarcely breath enough to work it free of a black root. But after three dives he had worked it loose and was surfacing again when he saw the bright water above him suddenly darken. He knew water too well to explain it, but held his breath longer and slowed his ascent until the darkness had passed by. Lucky it was, for when he broke through the foam, the giant body was gone past, its claws empty. All the fisherman saw clearly through water-filmed eyes was the great rudder of its red tail. He trod water by his boat, too frightened to pull himself in, and a minute later the dragon went over him again, its claws full of the innkeeper's prize bull, the one that had sired the finest calves in the countryside but was so fierce it had to be staked down day and night. The bull was still twitching and the blood fell from its back thicker than rain.

The fisherman slipped his hand from the boat and went under

61

the water, both to cleanse himself of the blood and the fear. When he surfaced again, the dragon was gone. But the fisherman stayed in the water until the cold at last drove him out, his hands as wrinkled as his grandpap's from their long soaking.

He swam to shore, forgetting both boat and line, and ran all the way back to the village leaving a wet trail. No one believed him until they saw the meadow from which the bull—chain and all—had been ripped. Then even the priest was convinced.

The healer's wife and her three daughters wept anew when they were told. And Tansy, remembering the patch of dragon's bane, blamed herself for not having guessed.

May-Ma raised her fist to the sky and screamed the old curse on dragons, remembered from years of mummery played out at planting:

Fire and water on thy wing,
The curse of God in beak and flight.

The priest tried to take the sting of her loss away. The cooper's wife was inconsolable as well, surrounded by her eleven younglings. The village men sharpened their iron pitchforks and the old poisoned arrows that hung on the church's small apse walls were heated until the venom dripped. Tansy had to treat three boys for the flux who had put their fingers on the arrows and then on their lips. The beekeeper got down an old book that had traveled through his family over the years called *Ye Draconis: An Historie Unnaturalis.* The only useful information therein was, "An fully fledged draconis will suppe and digeste an bullock in fourteen days." They counted twelve days at best before the beast returned to feed again.

And then someone said, "We need a dragonslayer."

———

So the fisherman's son and the beekeeper's son and three other boys were sent off to see who they could find, though the priest thundered from the pulpit, "Beware of false heroes. Without dragons there be no need of dragonslayers."

As the boys left the village, their neighbors gathered to bid them godspeed. The sexton rang Great Tom, the treble bell that had been cast in the hundredth year after the victory over dragons. On its side was the inscription *I am Tom, when I toll there is fire, when I thunder there is victory.* The boys carried the sound with them down the long, winding roads.

They found heroes aplenty in the towns they visited. There were men whose bravery extended to the rim of a wine cup but, sober the morning after, turned back into ploughboys, farmers, and laborers who sneaked home without a by-your-leave. They found one old general who remembered ancient wounds and would have followed them if he had had legs, but the man who carted him to and from town was too frightened to push the barrow after them. And they found a farmer's strong daughter who could lift a grown ewe under each arm but whose father forbade her to go. "One girl and five boys together on the road?" he roared. "Would that be proper? After such a trip, no one would wed her." So though she was a head taller than her da, and forty pounds heavier, she wanted a wedding, so she stayed.

It was in a tosspot inn that the five village boys found the one they sought. They knew him for a hero the moment he stood. He moved like a god, the golden hair rippling down his back. Muscles formed like small mountains on his arms and he could make them walk from shoulder to elbow without the slightest effort. He was of a clan of gentle giants but early on had had a longing to see the world.

It did not occur to any one of the five why a hero should have

63

sunk so low as to be cadging drinks by showing off his arms. It was enough for them that they had found him.

"Be you a hero?" breathed the fisherman's son, tracing the muscles with his eyes.

The blond man smiled, his teeth white and even. "Do I look like one?" he asked, answering question with question, making the muscles dance across his shoulders. "My name is Lancot."

The beekeeper's son looked dazzled. "That be a hero's name," he said with a sigh.

The boys shared their pennies and bought Lancot a mug of stew. He remembered things for them then: service to a foreign queen, a battle with a walking tree, three goblins spitted on his sword. (Their blood had so pitted the blade he left it on their common grave, which was why he had it not.) On and on through the night he spun out his tales and they doled out their coin in exchange. Each thought it a fair bargain.

In the morning they caught up with him several miles down the road, his pockets a-jangle with the coins they had paid for his tales—as well as the ones they thought they had gone to bed with. They begrudged him none of it. A hero is entitled.

"Come back with us, Lancot," begged the beekeeper's son, "and we can promise you a fine living."

"More coins than ten pockets could hold," added the fisherman's son, knowing it for a small boast.

They neglected to mention the dragon, having learned that one small lesson along the way.

And the hero Lancot judged them capable of five pockets at best. Still, five was better than none, and a fine village living was better than no living at all. There was bound to be at least one pretty girl there. He was weary of the road, for the world had turned out to be no better than his home—and no worse. So he shook his head, knowing that would make his golden hair ripple all down his back. And he tensed his muscles once more for good measure. They deserved *something* for their coin.

"He is almost like . . . a god," whispered one of the boys.

Lancot smiled to himself and threw his shoulders back. He looked straight ahead. He knew he was no god. He was not even, the gods help him, a hero. Despite his posture and his muscles, he was a fraud. Heroes and gods were never afraid and he was deadly afraid every day of his life. It was so absurd that he found himself laughing most of the time for, by holding himself upright and smiling his hero smile, by making others party to his monstrous fraud, he could keep most of the fears at bay.

And so they arrived home, the fisherman's son, the beekeeper's son, and the three other boys alternately trailing the golden-haired hero and leading him.

They were greeted by a sobbing crowd.

The dragon, it seems, had carried off the church bell ten days before. The sexton, who had been in the act of ringing matins, had clung to the rope and had been carried away as well. Great Tom had dropped upside down with a final dolorous knell into the bay, where it could still be seen. Little fish swam round its clapper. The sexton had not been found.

With all the sobbing and sighing, no one had noticed that the hero Lancot had turned the color of scum on an ocean wave. No one, that is, except Tansy, who noticed everything, and her sister Sage, who thought that gray-white was a wonderful tone for a hero's skin. "Like ice," she whispered to herself, "like the surface of a lake in winter, though his eyes are the color of a summer sky." And Rosemary, who thought he looked big enough and strong enough to train to the farm, much as a draft horse is measured for the plow.

As there was no inn and May-Ma had first claim on heroes, her husband having been the great worm's earliest meal, Lancot was put up at the healer's cottage. He eyed the three daughters with delight.

Their first dinner was a dismal affair. The healer's wife spoke of raw vengeance, Rosemary of working, Sage of romance, and Tansy of herbs. Lancot spoke not at all. In this place of dragons he knew he dared not tell his tales.

But finally Tansy took pity on his silence and asked him what, besides being a hero, he liked to do.

It being a direct question, Lancot had to answer. He thought a bit. Playing a hero had taken up all his adult time. At last he spoke. "When I was a boy . . ."

Sage sighed prettily, as if being a boy were the noblest occupation in the world.

"When I was a boy," Lancot said again, "I liked to fly kites."

"A useless waste of sticks and string," said Rosemary.

Sage sighed.

But as May-Ma cleared the table, Tansy nodded. "A link with earth and sky," she said. "As if you, too, were flying."

"If we were meant to fly," reminded Rosemary, "we would have been born with a beak . . ."

Sage laughed, a tinkling sound.

"And a longing for worms. Yes, I know," interrupted Tansy. "But little worms are useful creatures for turning the soil. It is only the great worms who are our enemies."

Rosemary's mouth thinned down.

Lancot said uneasily, "Kites . . ." then stopped. Dinner was over and the need for conversation was at an end.

———

In the morning the boys, backed up by their fathers, came to call. Morning being a hero's time, they came quite early. Lancot was still asleep.

"I will wake him," volunteered Sage. Her voice was so eager the fisherman's son bit his lip, for he had long loved her from afar.

Sage went into the back room and touched the sleeping hero on the shoulder. Lancot turned on the straw mattress but did not open his eyes.

"Never mind," said Rosemary urgently when Sage returned without him. "I shall do it."

She strode into the room and clapped her hands loudly right behind his left ear. Lancot sat up at once.

"Your followers are here," she snapped. "Tramping in mud and knocking the furniture about." She began to fluff up the pillow before the print of Lancot's head even had time to fade.

Reluctantly he rose, splashed drops of cold water on his cheeks, and went to face the boys.

"Do we go today?" asked the fisherman's son, quick to show his eagerness to Sage.

"Is it swords or spears?" asked the innkeeper's son.

"Or the poisoned arrows?"

"Or rocks?"

"Or . . ."

"Let me think," said Lancot, waving them into silence. "A dragon needs a plan."

"A plan," said all the boys and their fathers at once.

"Come back tomorrow and I will have a plan," said Lancot. "Or better yet, the day *after* tomorrow."

The boys nodded, but the beekeeper spoke timidly. "The day after tomorrow will be too late. The great worm is due to return to

feed. The sexton was . . ." he swallowed noisily, ". . . a puny man."
Unconsciously his hand strayed to his own ample waist.

Lancot closed his eyes and nodded as if he were considering a
plan, but what he was really thinking about was escape. When he
opened his eyes again, the boys and their fathers were gone. But
Rosemary was holding the broom in a significant manner, and so
Lancot put his head down as if in thought and strode from the house
without even worrying about breaking his fast.

He turned down the first wooded path he came to, which was
the path that wound down toward the river. He scarcely had time
for surprise when the wood opened into the broad, meandering water-
way, dotted with little isles, that at the edge of sight opened into
the sea. Between him and the river was a gentle marsh of reeds and
rice. Clustered white florets sat like tiny clouds upon green stems.
There was no boat.

"There you are," said Tansy, coming out of the woods behind
him. "I have found some perfect sticks for a kite and borrowed paper
from the priest. The paper has a recipe for mulberry wine on it, but
he says he has much improved the ingredients and so could let me
have it. And I have torn up Da's old smock for ribbons and plaited
vines for a rope."

"A kite?" Lancot said wonderingly. He stared at the girl, at her
river-blue eyes set in a face that seemed the color of planed wood.
Yesterday she had seemed no great beauty, yet here in the wood,
where she reflected the colors of earth, water, sky, she was beautiful
indeed. "A kite?" he asked again, his thoughts on her.

"Heroes move in mysterious ways," Tansy said, smiling. "And since
you mentioned kites, I thought perhaps kites were teasing into your
mind as part of your plan."

"My plan," Lancot repeated vaguely, letting his eyes grow misty as if in great thought. He was having trouble keeping his mind on heroics.

Suddenly he felt a touch on his hand, focused his eyes, and saw that Tansy had placed her green-stained fingers on his. *Her hands are like a wood sprite's,* he thought suddenly.

"Being a hero," Tansy said, "does not mean you need to be without fear. Only fools lack fear, and I believe you to be no fool."

He dared to look at her and whispered, "No hero, either." And having admitted it, he sank down on his heels as if suddenly free of shackles that had long held him upright.

Tansy squatted next to him. "I am no hero, either," she said. "To run away is by far the most sensible thing that either of us could do. But that will not stop this great worm from devouring my village and, ultimately, our world. The very least the two of us poor, frightened un-heroes can do is to construct a plan."

They sat for a long moment in silence, looking at one another. The woods stilled around them. Then Lancot smiled and, as if on a signal, the birds burst into full throat again. Little lizards resumed their scurrying. And over the water, sailing in lazy circles, a family of cormorants began their descent.

"A kite," said Lancot. His eyes closed with sudden memory. "I met a mage once, with strange high cheekbones and straw-colored hair. He spoke in a language that jangled the ear, and he told me that in his tongue the word for kite is *drache*, dragon."

Tansy nodded slowly. "Correspondences," she said. "It is the first rule of herbalry. Like calls to like. Like draws out like." She clapped her hands together. "I *knew* there was a reason that you spoke of kites."

"Do you mean that a kite could kill a dragon? *The* dragon?" Lancot asked. "Such a small, flimsy toy?"

Tansy laced her fingers together and put her chin down on top of her hands. "Not all by itself," she said. "But perhaps there is some way that we could manipulate the kite . . ."

"*I* could do that!" said Lancot.

"And use it to deliver a killing blow," Tansy finished.

"But there is no way a kite could carry a spear or bend a bow or wield a sword." Lancot paused. "You do not mean to fly *me* up on the kite to do that battle." He forgot to toss his hair or dance his muscles across his shoulders, so great was his fear.

Tansy laughed and put her hands on his knee. "Lancot, I have not forgotten that you are no hero. And I am no kite handler."

He furrowed his brow. "*You* will not go up the kite string. I forbid it."

"I am not yours to forbid," Tansy said quietly. "But I am no hero, either. What I had in mind was something else."

He stood then and paced while Tansy told him of her plan. The river rilled over rocks to the sea, and terns scripted warnings in the sky. Lancot listened only to the sound of Tansy's voice, and watched her fingers spell out her thoughts. When she finished, he knelt by her side.

"I will make us a great kite," he said. "A *drache*. I will need paint besides, red as blood and black as hope."

"I thought hope a lighter color," exclaimed Tansy.

"Not when one is dealing with dragons," he said.

The cooper supplied the paint. Two precious books of church receipts were torn apart for the paper because Lancot insisted that the kite be dragon size. The extra nappies belonging to the missing babe, the petticoats of six maidens, and the fisherman's son's favorite shirt were torn up for binding. And then the building began.

Lancot sent the boys into the woods for spruce saplings after refusing to make his muscles dance. They left sullenly with his caveat in their ears: "As the dragon is mighty, yet can sail without falling through the air, so must the wood of our kite likewise be strong yet light."

Tansy, overhearing this, nodded and muttered, "Correspondences," under her breath.

And then the hero, on his knees, under the canopy of trees, showed them how to bend the wood, soaking it in water to make it flex, binding it with the rags. He ignored the girls who stood behind him to watch his shoulders ripple as he worked.

The fisherman's son soon got the hang of it, as did the cooper's eldest daughter. Rosemary was best, grumbling at the waste of good cloth, but also proud that her fingers could so nimbly wrap the wood.

They made rounded links, the first twice as large as a man, then descending in size to the middle whose circumference was that of Great Tom's bow. From there the links became smaller till the last was a match for the priest's dinner plate.

"We could play at rings," suggested Sage brightly. Only the fisherman's son laughed.

All the while Tansy sat crosslegged, plaiting a rope. She used the trailing vines that snaked down from the trees and added horsehair that she culled from the local herd. She borrowed hemp and line from the fisherman's wife, but she did the braiding herself, all the while whispering a charm against the unknitting of bones.

It took a full day, but at last the links were made and stacked and Lancot called the villagers to him. "Well done," he said, patting the smallest boy on the head. Then he sent the lot of them home.

Only Tansy remained behind. "That was indeed well done," she said.

"It was *easy* done," he said. "There is nothing to fear in the making of a kite. But once *it* is finished, I will be gone."

71

"A hero does what a hero can," answered Tansy. "We ask no more than that." But she did not stop smiling, and Lancot took up her smile as his own.

They walked along the path together toward the house but, strange to say, they were both quite careful not to let their hands meet or to let the least little bit of their clothing touch. They only listened to the nightjar calling and the erratic beating of their own timid hearts.

The next morning, before the sun had picked out a path through the interlacing of trees, the villagers had assembled the links into the likeness of a great worm. Lancot painted a dragon's face on the largest round and colored in the rest like the long, sinewy body and tail.

The boys placed the poisoned arrowheads along the top arch of the links like the ridge of a dragon's neck. The girls tied sharpened sticks beneath, like a hundred unsheathed claws.

Then the priest blessed the stick-and-paper beast, saying:

Fly with the hopes of men to guide you,
Fly with the heart of a hero to goad you,
Fly with the spirit of God to guard you,
    Blessings on you, beak and tail.

Tansy made a hole in the *drache*'s mouth, which she hemmed with a white ribbon from her own hope chest. Through that hole she strung a single long red rope. To one end of the rope she knotted a reed basket; to the other she looped a handle.

"What is the basket for?" asked May-Ma. "Why do we do this? Where will it get us? And will it bring dear Da back home?"

Rosemary and Sage comforted her, but only Tansy answered her. "It is the hero's plan," she said.

And with that May-Ma and all the villagers, whose own questions had rested in hers, had to be content.

Then with all the children holding the links, they marched down to the farthest shore. There, on the strand, where the breezes shifted back and forth between one island and the next, they stretched out the great kite, link after link, along the sand.

Lancot tested the strings, straightening and untwisting the line. Then he wound up the guy string on Rosemary's shuttle. Looking up into the sky, one hand over his eyes, he saw that for miles there were no clouds. Even the birds were down. It was an elegant slate on which to script their challenge to the great worm.

"Links up!" he cried. And at that signal, the boys each grabbed a large link, the girls the smaller ones, and held them over their heads.

"Run from me," Lancot cried.

And the children began to run, pulling the great guy rope taut between them as they went.

Meanwhile Lancot and the village men held fast to the unwinding end, tugging it up and over their own heads.

Then the wind caught the links, lifting them into the air, till the last, smallest part of the tail was up. And the beekeeper's littlest daughter, who was holding it, was so excited she forgot to let go and was carried up and away.

"I will catch you," cried the fisherman's son to her, and she let go after a bit and fell into his arms. Sage watched admiringly and touched him on the arm, and he was so red with hope he let the child tumble out of his hands.

The wind fretted and goaded the kite, and the links began to swim through the air, faster and higher, in a sinuous dance; up over their outstretched hands, over the tops of trees, until only the long red rope curling from the mouth lay circling both ends on the ground.

"Make it fast," commanded Lancot, and the men looped the great guy around the trunk of an old, thick willow, once, twice, and then a third time for luck. Then the fisherman knotted the end and the priest threw holy water on it.

"And now?" asked Rosemary.

"And now?" asked the priest.

"And now?" echoed the rest of the villagers.

"And now you must all run off home and hide," said Lancot, for it was what Tansy had rehearsed with him. "The dragon will be here within the day."

"But what is the basket for?" asked May-Ma. "And why do we do this? And where will it get us? And will it bring your dear da back?" This last she asked to Tansy, who was guiding her down the path.

But there were no answers and so no comfort in it. All the villagers went home. Tansy alone returned to find Lancot pacing by the shore.

"I thought you would be gone," she said.

"I will be." His voice was gruff, but it broke between each word.

"Then the next work is mine," said Tansy.

"I will help." His eyes said there would be no argument.

He followed her along the shoreline till they came to the place where the river flowed out, the blue-white of the swift-running water meeting the lapis of the sea. Tansy turned upstream, wading along the water's edge. That left Lancot either the deeper water or the sand. He chose the water.

Tansy questioned him with a look.

He shrugged. "I would not have you fall in," he said.

"I can swim," she answered.

"I cannot."

She laughed and skipped onto the sand. Relieved, Lancot followed.

Suddenly Tansy stopped. She let slip the pocket of woven reeds she had tied at her waist. "Here," she said, pointing.

Between the sturdy brown cattails and the spikes of wild rice was a strangely sown pattern of grassy weeds, bloody red in color, the tops embroidered with florets of pearl and pink.

"*That* is dragon's bane?" Lancot asked. "That pretty bouquet? *That* is for our greatest need?" He snorted and bent and brushed a finger carelessly across one petal. The flower seared a bloody line across his skin. "Ow!" he cried and stuck the finger in his mouth.

"Best put some aloe on that," Tansy said, digging around in her apron pocket.

Lancot shook his head. Taking his finger from his mouth he said quickly, "No bother. It is just a little sting." Then he popped the finger back in.

Tansy laughed. "I have brought my mitts this time. Fireweed burns only flesh. I, too, have felt that sting." She held up her hand and he could see a string of little rounded, faded scars across her palm. "Dragons are made of flesh—under the links of mail."

Lancot reached out with his burned finger and touched each scar gently, but he did not say a word.

Taking her mitts from a deep apron pocket, Tansy drew them on. Then she grasped the fireweed stems with one hand, the flowers with the other, and snapped the blossoms from the green stalk. Little wisps of smoke rose from her mitts, but did not ignite. She put each cluster into her bag.

Lancot merely watched, alert, as if ready to help.

At last the bag was pouched full of flowers.

"It is enough," Tansy said, stripping the mitts from her hands.

Back at the beach, Tansy lowered the flying basket carefully and stuffed it full of the bane. As she hauled on the rope, sending the basket back aloft, a steady stream of smoke poured through the wicker, a hazy signal written on the cloudless sky.

"Now we wait," said Tansy.

"Now we wait *under cover*," said Lancot. He led her to a nearby narrow gulch and pulled branches of willow across from bank to bank. Then he slipped under the branches, pulling Tansy after.

"Will we have to wait long?" Tansy mused, more to herself than to Lancot.

Before he could answer, they heard a strange loud chuffing, a foreign wind through the trees, and smelled a carrion stink. And though neither of them had ever heard that sound before or smelled that smell, there was no mistaking it.

"Dragon," breathed Lancot.

"*Vermifax major*," said Tansy.

And then the sky above them darkened as the great mailed body, its stomach links scratched and bloodstained from lying on old bones, put out their sun.

Instinctively, they both cringed beneath the lacy willow leaves until the red rudder of tail sailed over. Tansy even forgot to breathe, so that when the worm was gone from sight and only the smell lingered, she drew a deep breath and nearly choked on the stench. Lancot clapped his hand so hard over her mouth he left four marks on the left side of her face and a red thumbprint high on the right cheekbone. Her only protest was to place her hand gently on his wrist.

"Oh, Tansy, forgive me, I am sorry I hurt you." Lancot bit his lip. "My strength is greater than I supposed."

"I am not sorry," she answered back. "This"—she brushed her fingers across her face—"this is but a momentary pain. If that great beast had heard me and had hurt you, the pain would go on and on and on forever."

At that moment they heard a tremendous angry scream of defiance and a strange rattling sound.

"The dragon must have seen our kite," whispered Tansy.

"And like all great single beasts, he kills what he cannot court."

Lancot shifted a willow branch aside with great care, and they both blinked in the sudden light of sky. High above them the red dragon was challenging the *drache*, voice and tail making statements that no self-respecting stranger would leave unanswered. But the kite remained mute.

The dragon screamed again and dived at the kite's smallest links, severing the last two. As the links slipped through the air, twisting and spiraling in the drafts made by the dragon's wings, the beast turned on the paper-and-stick pieces and swallowed them in a single gulp. Then, with a great surprised belch, the worm vomited up the pieces again. Crumpled, broken, mangled beyond repair, they fell straight down into the sea.

The dragon roared again, this time snapping at the head of the kite. The roar was a mighty wind that whipped the kite upward, and so the dragon's jaws closed only on the rope that held the basket of fireweed, shredding the strand. The basket and half the rope fell lazily through the air and, with a tiny splash, sank beneath the waves. At once, a high frantic hissing bubbled up through the water, and the sea boiled with the bane.

"It's gone," Tansy whispered. "The bane. It's gone." Without giving a thought for her own safety, she clambered out of the gulch and, bent over, scuttled to the trees, intent on fetching more of the precious weed. The dragon, concentrating on its skyborne foe, never saw her go.

But Lancot did, his hand reaching out too late to clutch the edge of her skirt as it disappeared over the embankment. "Tansy, no!"

She made no sign she had heard, but entered the trees and followed the stream quickly to the muddle of water and reeds that held the rest of the bane. Wading in, she began to snatch great handfuls of the stuff, heedless of the burns, until she had gathered all there was to find. Then she struggled ashore and raced back. Her wet skirts tangled in her legs as she ran.

Lancot, caught in a panic of indecision, had finally emerged from their hiding place and stared alternately at the sky and the path along the sea. When Tansy came running back, hands seared and smoking but holding the fireweed, he ran to her.

"I have gathered all there is," she said, only at the last letting her voice crack with the pain.

Lancot reached for the weed.

"No," Tansy whispered hoarsely, "take the mitts from my pocket." She added miserably, "I was in such a hurry, I forgot to put them on. And then I was in too much pain to do other."

Lancot grabbed the mitts from her pocket and forced them onto his large hands. Then he took the weed from her. She hid her burned hands behind her back.

"How will I get these up to the dragon?" asked Lancot suddenly, for the question had not occurred to either of them before.

They turned as one and stared at the sky.

It was the dragon itself that gave them the answer then, for, as they watched, it grabbed a great mouthful of the kite and raged at it, pulling hard against the line that tethered the *drache* to the tree. The willow shook violently with each pull.

Lancot smiled down at Tansy. "You are no hero," he said. "Your hands are too burned for that. And I am no hero, either. But . . ." His voice trembled only slightly. "As a boy I fetched many kites out of trees." And before Tansy could stop him, he kissed her forehead, careful of the bane he carried, and whispered into her hair, "And put some *hallow* on those palms."

"Aloe," she said, but he did not hear her.

Lancot transferred the bane to one mitt, slipped the mitt off his other hand, and began to shinny one-handed up the guy rope that was anchored to the underside of the kite. If the dragon, still wrestling with the *drache*, felt the extra weight, it made not the slightest sign.

Twice the dragon pulled so furiously that Lancot slipped off. And then, when he was halfway up the rope, there was a huge sucking sound. Slowly the willow was pulled up, roots and all, out of the earth. And the dragon, along with the kite, the string, Lancot, and the tree, flew east toward the farthest isles.

Tansy, screaming and screaming, watched them go.

As they whipped through the air, Lancot continued his slow crawl up the rope. Once or twice the fireweed brushed his cheek and he gritted his teeth against the pain. And once a tiny floret touched his hair, and the single strand sizzled down to his scalp. The smell of that was awful. But he did not drop the weeds nor did he relinquish his hold on the guy. Up and up he inched as the dragon, its limp paper prey in its claws, pulled them toward its home.

They were closing in on the farthest island, a sandy lozenge shape resting in the blue sea, when Lancot's bare hand touched the bottom of the kite and the cold golden nail of the dragon's claw. He could feel his heart hammering hard against his chest and the skin rippled faster along his shoulders and neck than ever he could have made the muscles dance. He could feel the wind whistling past his bared teeth, could feel the tears teasing from his eyes. He remembered Tansy's voice saying "I can swim," and his own honest reply. Smiling ruefully, he thought, "I shall worry about that anon." Then he slipped his arm around the dragon's leg, curved his legs up and around, until he could kneel. He dared not look down again.

He stood and at last the dragon seemed to take notice of him. It clenched and unclenched its claw. The kite and tree fell away, tumbling, it seemed, forever till they plunged into the sea, sending up a splash that could be seen from all the islands.

Lancot looked up just in time to see the great head of the beast bend curiously around to examine its own feet. It was an awkward move in the air, and for a moment worm and man plummeted downward.

Then the dragon opened its great furnace jaws, the spikes of teeth as large as tree trunks, as sharp as swords.

Lancot remembered his boyhood and the games of sticks and balls. He snatched up the fireweed with his ungloved hand and, ignoring the sting of it, flung the lot into the dragon's maw.

Surprised, the dragon swallowed, then straightened up and began to roar.

Lancot was no fool. He put the mitt over his eyes, held his nose with his burned hand, and jumped.

On shore, Tansy had long since stopped screaming to watch the precarious climb. Each time Lancot slipped she felt her heart stutter. She prayed he might drop off before the dragon noticed, until she remembered he could not swim.

When he reached the dragon's foot, Tansy was wading into the water, screaming once again. Her aloe-smeared hands had left marks on her skirts, on her face.

And when the tree and kite fell, she felt her hopes rise until she saw that Lancot was not with them. She prayed then, the only prayer she could conjure up, the one her mother had spoken:

Fire and water on thy wing,
The curse of God in beak and flight.

It seemed to her much too small a prayer to challenge so great and horrible a beast.

81

And then the dragon turned on itself, curling around to look at Lancot, and they began to tumble toward the sea.

At that point Tansy no longer knew what prayers might work. "Fly!" she screamed. "Drop!" she screamed.

No sooner had she called out the last than the dragon straightened out and roared so loudly she had to put her hands over her ears, heedless of the aloe smears in her hair. Then, as she watched, the great dragon began to burn. Its body seemed touched by a red aureole and flames flickered the length of it, from mouth to tail. Quite suddenly, it seemed to go out, guttering like a candle, from the back forward. Black scabs fell from its tail, its legs, its back, its head. It turned slowly around in the air, as if each movement brought pain, and then Tansy could see its head. Only its eyes held life till the very end when, with a blink, the life was gone. The dragon drifted, floated down onto a sandbar, and lay like a mountain of ash. It was not a fierce ending but rather a gigantic sigh, and Tansy could not believe how unbearably sad it made her feel, as if she and the dragon and Lancot, too, had been cheated of some reward for their courage. She thought, quite suddenly, of a child's balloon at a fair pricked by a needle, and she wept.

A hand on her shoulder recalled her to the place. It was the fisherman's son.

"Gone then?" he asked. He meant the dragon.

But knowing Lancot was gone as well, Tansy began sobbing anew. Neither her mother nor her sisters nor the priest nor all the celebrations that night in the town could salve her. She walked down to the water's edge at dusk by herself and looked out over the sea to the spit of land where the ash mound that had been the dragon was black against the darkening sky.

The gulls were still. From behind her a solitary owl called its place from tree to tree. A small breeze teased into the willows, setting them to rustling. Tansy heard a noise near her and shrugged further into herself. She would let no one pull her out of her misery, not her mother nor her sisters nor all the children of the town.

"I could use a bit of *hallow* on my throwing hand," came a voice.

"Aloe," she said automatically before she turned.

"It's awfully hard to kill a hero," said Lancot with a smile.

"But you can't swim."

"It's low tide," he said. "And I *can* wade."

Tansy laughed.

"It's awfully hard to kill a hero," so said Lancot. "But we ordinary fellows, we do get hurt. So I could use a bit of *hallow* on my hand."

She didn't mind the smear of aloe on her hair and cheek. But that came later on, much later that night. And it seemed to the two of them that what they did then was very heroic indeed.

There is a spit of land near the farthest shores of the farthest islands. It is known as Dragonfield. Once dragons dwelt on the isles in great herds, feeding on the dry brush and fueling their flames with the carcasses of small animals and migratory birds. There are no dragons there now, though the nearer islands are scored with long furrows as though giant claws had been at work, and the land is fertile from the bones of the buried behemoths. There is a large mount of ash-colored rock that appears and disappears in the ebb and flow of the tide. No birds land on that rock, and seals avoid it as well. The islanders call it Worm's Head, and once a year they row out to it and sail a great kite from its highest point, a kite that they then set afire and let go into the prevailing winds. Some of the younger mothers complain that one day that kite will burn down a house, and they have agitated to end the ceremony. But as long as the story of Tansy and the hero is told, the great kites will fly over the rock, of that I am sure.

This story began as a joke. I had written down a list of titles, brainstorming and playing word associations one day when I had no ideas in my head. It was a kind of mental exercise, and the title "Dragon—or Dragoon" surfaced. That list existed for fully fifteen years before I ever tried to create a story that included both a dragon and a dragoon.

"The King's Dragon" happened because I was trying to write an extremely tellable story, one I could perform on stage. I remembered the opening of "Stone Soup" and used it quite consciously for the beginning of my own tale.

The King's Dragon

There was once a soldier who had fought long and hard for his king. He had been wounded in the war and sent home for a rest.

Hup and one. Hup and two. He marched down the long, dusty road, using a crutch.

He was a member of the Royal Dragoons. His red-and-gold uniform was dirty and torn. And in the air of the winter's day, his breath plumed out before him like a cloud.

Hup and one. Hup and two. Wounded or not, he marched with a proud step. For the Royal Dragoons are the finest soldiers in the land and—they always obey orders.

After a bit, the soldier came upon a small village. House after house nestled together in a line.

"Just the place to stop for the night," thought the dragoon to himself. So he hupped and one, hupped and two, up to the door of the very first house. He blew the dust from his uniform, polished the medals on his chest with his sleeve till they clinked and clanked together and shone like small suns. Then he knocked on the door with his crutch.

Now that very first house belonged to a widow and she, poor woman, was slightly deaf. When she finally heard the sound of the knock, she called out in a timid voice, "Who is there?"

The soldier puffed out his chest. He struck his crutch smartly on the ground. "I am a Royal Dragoon," he said, "and I am tired and hungry and would like to come in."

The woman began to shake. "The royal *dragon?*" she cried, for she had not heard him clearly. "I did not know the king had one. But if it *is* a dragon, and hungry besides, I certainly do not want him here. For he will eat up all I have and me as well!" She so frightened herself that she threw her apron up over her head and called out, *"Go away!"* Then weeping and wailing, she ran out her back door to her neighbor's home.

The Royal Dragoon did not see her leave, of course. But as she had told him to go, go he did, for the Royal Dragoons are the finest soldiers in the land and—they always obey orders.

Hup and one. Hup and two. He marched to the second house and knocked on the door. He stood at attention, his chest puffed out, and in the cold, wintry air, his breath plumed out before him like a cloud.

Now that second house belonged to the widow's father, and he, poor man, was nearly blind. He listened to his daughter's story, and when the knock came, the two of them crept up to the window. She still had her apron up over her head, and he could see no farther than the end of his nose. They peered out, and all they saw was the great plume of breath coming from the soldier's mouth.

"See," said the daughter, "it *is* a dragon. And he is breathing smoke."

"Who is there?" called out the old man in a timid voice.

"I am a Royal Dragoon," said the soldier. As he spoke, even more clouds streamed from his mouth. "I am tired and hungry and would like to come in."

"*Go away!*" cried the old man. "No one is here." Then he and his daughter ran out the back way to their neighbor's house, weeping as they went.

The Royal Dragoon did not see them leave, of course. But as he had been told to go, go he did, for the Royal Dragoons are the finest soldiers in the land and—they always obey orders.

Hup and one. Hup and two. He marched to the third house and knocked on the door. He stood at attention, his chest puffed out, and saluted so smartly his medals clinked and clanked together.

Now the third house belonged to the mayor, and a very smart young mayor he was. He could see perfectly well. He could hear perfectly well. And when the widow and her father finished their story, the mayor said: "The king's dragon, eh? And just listen to that! I hear his scales clinking and clanking together. He must be terribly hungry indeed and ready to pounce."

So the mayor called out the door, "*Wait,* Sir Dragon." Then the mayor and the widow and the widow's father ran out the back. They gathered together all the other people in the town, and without even taking time to pick up their belongings, they ran and ran as fast as they could, until they came to the mountains, where a very real dragon lived. When it came out and ate them all up, not a one of them was surprised. They were already convinced of dragons, you see.

As for the Royal Dragoon, he stood waiting at attention in front of the third house for a very, very, very long time. He may be standing there still. For the Royal Dragoons are the finest soldiers in the land. And—they always obey orders.

I give a lot of speeches: speeches to schools, speeches to libraries, speeches to college classes, speeches to groups of teachers, librarians, storytellers, and would-be writers.

One day I was asked to give a speech to a group called the Mythopoeic Society. It is an organization dedicated to fantasy literature, especially to the works of such writers as J. R. R. Tolkien and C. S. Lewis—two of my favorite authors. This was the national conference, and the weekend was called "The Wood Between the Worlds." I wrote this poem to end my speech.

Into the Wood

Let us enter the wood.
Take my hand.
I feel your fear
rise on your palm,
a map beneath my fingers.
Can you decipher
the pulsing code
that beats at my wrist?
I do not need to see
dragons
to know there are
dragons here.
The back of my neck knows,
the skin of my inner thighs.
There, among the alders,
between twin beeches,
the gray-white pilasters

twined with wild grape,
stands a pavilion,
inferior Palladian in style.
Who sleeps on the antique couch?
I hear a thin scraping,
a belly through dead leaves,
a long, hollow good-bye,
thin, full of scales,
modal, descending sounds.
In the dark
there will be eyes
thick as starshine,
a galaxy of watchers
beneath the trailing vine.
And trillium,
the red of heart's blood,
spills between rocks
to mark the path.
Do not, for God's sake,
let my hand go.
Do not, for God's sake,
speak.
I know what is here
and what is not,
and if we do not
name it aloud
it will do us no harm.
So the spells go,
so the tales go,
and I must believe it so.

My husband calls this story "King Arthur Meets the Wizard of Oz" and I think he is right. After you read it, you will understand why.

It is one of almost a dozen stories I originally wrote about Merlin for a collection called Merlin's Booke.

I was fascinated by the father-son relationship between Merlin and Arthur, but also interested in how we pass on our knowledge and our family stories. But when I finished the short story, I wasn't entirely finished with the idea. Several years later, while living in Scotland, I rewrote the story into a novel of the same name.

Another more personal thing informed this story. I worked on it when my father, dying of Parkinson's disease, had an apartment in our farmhouse. One day I went in to check up on him and he was fast asleep, his mouth slightly open. Over the years I had tried to please my father and had so often failed. This time he looked so old and vulnerable, I thought out loud: "The dragon has no teeth." And from that moment on I was easier with him than I had ever been. Stories are like that.

The Dragon's Boy

It was on a day in early spring with the clouds scudding across a gray sky that the boy found the cave. He had been chasing after Lord Ector's brachet hound, the one who always slipped her chain to go after hare. She had slipped him as well, leaving him lost in the boggy wasteland north of the castle walls. He had crossed and re-crossed a small, meandering stream, following her, wading thigh-deep in water that—he was painfully aware of it—would only come up to the other boys' knees. The reminder of his height only made him crankier.

The sun was high, his stomach empty, and the brachet had quit baying an hour earlier. She was no doubt back at the kennel yard, slopping up her food. But she was his responsibility, and he had to stay out until he was sure. Besides, he was lost. Well, not exactly lost but *bothered* a bit, which was a phrase he had picked up from the master of hounds, a whey-colored man for all that he was out of doors most of the day.

The boy looked around for a place to get out of the noon sun, for the low, hummocky swamp with its brown pools and quaking mosses offered little shelter. And then he saw a small tor mounding up over the bog. He decided to climb it a bit to see if he could find a place where he might shelter, maybe even survey the land. He'd never been quite this far from the castle on his own before and certainly had never come out into the northern fens where the peat-hags reigned, and he needed time to think about the way home. And the brachet. If the mound had been higher, he wouldn't have attempted it. The High Tor, the really large mound northwest of the manor, had somewhat of an evil reputation. But this hillock was hardly that. He needed to get his bearings and sight the castle walls or at least a tower.

He was halfway up the tor when he saw the cave.

It was only an unprepossessing black hole in the rock, as round as if it had been carved and then smoothed by a master hand. He stepped in, being careful of the long, spearlike hanging rocks, and let his eyes get used to the dark. Only then did he hear the breathing. It was not very loud, but it was steady and rumbling, with an occasional *pop!* that served as punctuation.

He held his breath and began to back out of the cave, hit his head on something that rang in twenty different tones, and said a minor curse under his breath.

"Staaaaaaaaaaay," came a low command.

He stopped. And so, for a stuttering moment, did his heart.

"Whoooooooooo are you?" It was less an echo bouncing off cave walls than an elongated sigh.

The boy bit his lip and answered in a voice that broke several times in odd places. "I am nobody. Just Artos. A fosterling from the castle." Then he added hastily, "Sir."

A low rumbling sound, more like a snore than a sentence, was all that was returned to him. It was that homey sound that freed him of his terror long enough to ask, "And who are you?" He hesitated. "Sir."

Something creaked. There was a strange clanking. Then the voice, augmented almost tenfold, boomed at him, "I am the Great Riddler. I am the Master of Wisdoms. I am the Word and I am the Light. I Was and Am and Will Be."

Artos nearly fainted from the noise. He put his right hand before him as if to hold back the sound. When the echoes had ended, he said in a quiet little voice, "Are you a hermit, sir? An anchorite? Are you a druid? A penitent knight?"

The great whisper that answered him came in a rush of wind. "I am The Dragon."

"Oh," said Artos.

"Is that all you can say?" asked the dragon. "I tell you I am The Dragon and all you can answer is *oh*?"

The boy was silent.

The great breathy voice sighed. "Sit down, boy. It has been a long time since I have had company in my cave. A long time and a lonely time."

"But . . . but . . . but." It was not a good beginning.

"No *buts*," said the dragon.

"But . . . ," Artos began again, needing greatly to uphold his end of the conversation.

"Shush, boy, and listen. I will pay for your visit."

The boy sat. It was not greed that stayed him. Rather, he was comforted by the thought that he was not to be eaten.

"So, Artos, how would you like your payment? In gold, in jewels, or in wisdom?"

A sudden flame from the center of the cave lit up the interior and, for the first time, Artos could see that there were jewels scattered about the floor as thick as pebbles. But dragons were known to be great game players. Cunning, like an old habit, claimed the boy. Like most small people, he had a genius for escape. "Wisdom, sir," he said.

Another bright flame spouted from the cave center. "An excellent choice," said the dragon. "I've been needing a boy just your age to pass my wisdom on to. So listen well."

Artos did not move and hoped that the dragon would see by his attitude that he was listening.

"My word of wisdom for the day is this: Old dragons, like old thorns, can still prick. And I am a very old dragon. Take care."

"Yes, sir," said Artos, thinking but not saying that that was a bit of wit often spoken on the streets of the village nestled inside the castle walls. But the warning by the villagers was of priests and thorns, not dragons. Aloud he said, "I will remember. Sir."

"Go now," said the dragon. "And as a reward for being such a good listener, you may take that small jewel. There." The strange clanking that Artos had heard before accompanied the extension of a gigantic foot with four enormous toes, three in the front and one in the back. It scrabbled along the cave floor, then stopped not far from Artos. Then the nail from the center toe extended peculiarly and tapped on a red jewel the size of a leek bulb.

Artos moved cautiously toward the jewel and the claw. Hesitating a moment, he suddenly leaned over and grabbed up the jewel. Then he scuttered back to the cave entrance.

93

"I will expect you tomorrow," said the dragon. "You will come during your time off."

"How did you know I had time off?" asked Artos.

"When you have become as wise as a dragon, you will know these things."

Artos sighed.

"There is a quick path from the back bridge. Discover it. And you will bring me stew. With *meat*!" The nail was suddenly sheathed and, quite rapidly, the foot was withdrawn into the dark center of the cave.

"To-tomorrow," promised the boy, not meaning a word of it.

The next morning at the smithy, caught in the middle of a quarrel between Old Linn the apothecary and Magnus Pieter the swordmaker, Artos was reminded of his promise. He had not forgotten the dragon—indeed the memory of the great clanking scales, the giant claw, the shaft of searing breath, the horrendous whisper had haunted his dreams. But he had quite conveniently forgotten his promise, or shunted it aside, or buried it behind layers of caution, until the argument had broken out.

"But there is never any *meat* in my gravy," whined Old Linn.

"Nor any meat in your manner," replied the brawny smith. "Nor were you mete for battle." The smith rather fancied himself a wordsman as well as a swordsman. And until Old Linn had had a fit, falling face first into his soup in the middle of entertaining the visiting high king, the smith had been spitted regularly by Old Linn's quick tongue. Now Linn was too slow for such ragging and he never told tales after meals anymore. It was said he had lost the heart for it after his teeth had left prints on the table. But he was kept on at the castle because Lord Ector had a soft heart and a long memory. And because—so backstair gossip had it—Linn had a cupboard full of strange herbs locked up behind doors covered with deep-carved runes.

Artos, who had been at the smithy to try and purchase a sword with his red jewel, was caught with his bargaining only just begun. He had not even had time to show the gem to Magnus Pieter when Old Linn had shambled in and, without any prelude, started his whining litany. His complaints were always laid at the smith's door. No one else in the castle was as old as the pair of them. Not even Lord Ector. They were best of friends by their long and rancorous association.

"My straw is ne'er changed but once a se'nnight," Linn complained. "My slops are ne'er emptied. I am given the dregs of the wine to drink. And now I must sit, if I am to be welcomed at all, well below the salt."

The smith smiled and returned to tapping on his piece of steel. He had stopped when Artos had begun his inquiries. In time to the beat of the hammer, he said, "But you have straw, though you no longer earn it. And a pot for your slops, which you can empty yourself. You have wine, even though you ne'er pay for it. And even below the salt, there is gravy in your bowl."

That was when Old Linn had whined piteously, "But there is never any *meat* in my gravy."

It was the word *meat* and Magnus Pieter's seven or eight variations on it that rung like a knell in Artos's head. For *meat* had been the dragon's final word.

He slunk off without even the promise of a sword, that shining piece of steel that might make him an equal in the eyes of the other boys, the gem still burning brightly in his tightly clenched hand.

He brought a small pot of gravy with three pieces of meat with him. Strolling casually out the back gate as if he had all the time in the world, nodding slightly at the guards over the portcullis, Artos could feel his heartbeat quicken. He had walked rather more quickly over the moat bridge, glancing at the gray-green water where the old moat tortoise lazed atop the rusted crown of a battle helm. Once he was across, however, he began to run.

It was difficult not to spill the stew, but he managed. The path was a worn thread through a wilderness of peat mosses and tangled brush. He even clambered over two rock outcroppings in the path that were studded with stones that looked rather like lumps of meat themselves. And, actually, climbing over the rocks was easier than wheedling the pot of stew had been. He only had it because Mag the scullion was sweet on him and he had allowed her to kiss him full on the lips. She hadn't noticed how he had held his breath, hoping to avoid the stink of her garlic, and closed his eyes not to see her bristly mustache. And she sighed so much after the kiss she hadn't had time to ask what he needed the stew for. But what if the dragon wanted gravy every day and he had to give Mag more kisses? It didn't bear thinking about, so Artos thought instead about the path. The dragon had been right. There was a quicker route back to the mound. Its only disadvantages were the two large rocks and the old thorny briar bushes. But they, at least, were safer than the peat pools which held bones enough way far down.

He got to the cave rather more quickly than he had bargained. Breathless, he squinted into the dark hole. This time he heard no heavy dragon breathing.

"Maybe," he said aloud to himself, his own voice lending him badly needed courage, "there's no one home. So I can just leave the gravy—and go."

"Staaaaaaaaay," came the sudden rumbling.

Artos almost dropped the pot.

"I have the gravy," he shouted quickly. He hadn't meant to be so loud, but fear always made him either too quiet or too loud. He was never sure which it was to be.

"Then give it meeeeeeeee," said the voice, followed by the clanking as the great claw extended halfway into the cave.

Artos could tell it was the foot by its long shadow. This time there was no stream of fire, only a hazy smoldering light from the back of the cave. Feeling a little braver then, he said, "I shall need to take the pot back with me. Sir."

"You shall take a bit of wisdom instead," came the voice.

Artos wondered if it would make him wise enough to avoid Mag's sweaty embrace. Somehow he doubted it.

"Tomorrow you shall have the pot. When you bring me more."

"More?" This time Artos's voice squeaked.

"Moooooooore," said the dragon. "With meat!" The nail extended, just as it had the day before, and caught under the pot handle. There was a horrible screeching as the pot was lifted several inches into the air, then slowly withdrawn into the recesses of the cave. There were strange scrabbling noises as if the dragon were sorting through its possessions, and then the clanking resumed. The claw returned and dropped something at Artos's feet.

He looked down. It was a book, rather tatty around the edges, he thought, though in the cave light it was hard to be sure.

"Wissssssssdom," said the dragon.

Artos shrugged. "It's just a book. I know my letters. Father Bertram taught me."

"Letterssssss turn matter into ssssssspirit," hissed the dragon.

"You mean it's a book of magic?"

"All booksssss are magic, boy." The dragon sounded just a bit cranky.

"Well, I can read," said Artos, stooping to pick up the book. He added a quick, "Thank you," thinking he should seem grateful. *Old thorns and old dragons . . .* he reminded himself.

"You can read *letters*, my boy, which is more than I can say for your castle contemporaries. And you can read *words*. But you must learn to read *inter linea*, between the lines."

Edging backward to the cave's mouth, Artos opened the book and scanned the first page. His fingers underlined each word; his mouth formed them. He turned the page. Then he looked up puzzled. "There is nothing written between the lines. Sir."

Something rather like a chuckle crossed with a cough echoed from the cave. "There is always something written between the lines. But it takes great wisdom to read it."

"Then why me, sir? I have little wisdom."

"Because . . . because you are here."

"Here?"

"Today. And not back at Ector's feeding his brachet or cleaning out the mews or sweating in the smithy or fighting with that pack of unruly boys. Here. For the getting of wisdom." The dragon made stretching noises.

"Oh."

There was a sudden tremendous wheezing and clanking and a strange, "Oh-oh," from the dragon.

Artos peered into the back of the cave nervously. It was all darkness and shadow and an occasional finger of firelight. "Are you all right? Sir?"

A long silence followed during which Artos wondered whether he should go to the dragon. He wondered if he had even the smallest amount of wisdom needed to help out. Then, just as he was about to make the plunge, the dragon's voice came hissing back. "Yesssssss, boy."

"Yes what, sir?"

"Yesssssss I am all right."

"Well, then," said Artos, putting one foot quietly behind the other, "thank you for my wisdom."

A furious flame spat across the cave, leaping through the darkness to lick Artos's feet. He jumped back, startled at the dragon's accuracy and suddenly hideously afraid. Had it just been preparation for the dragon's dinner after all? He suddenly wished for the sword he had not yet purchased, turned, and ran out of the cave.

The dragon's voice followed him. "Ssssssssilly child. That was not the wisdom."

From a safe place alongside the outside wall of the cave, Artos peeked in. "There's more?" he asked.

"By the time I am through with you, Artos Pendragon, Arthur son of the dragon, you will read *inter linea* in people as well." There was a loud moan and another round of furious clanking, and then total silence.

Taking it as a dismissal and holding the book hard against his chest, Artos ran down the hill. Whatever else he thought about as he neared the castle walls, topmost in his mind was what he would tell Mag about the loss of the gravy pot. It might mean another kiss. That was the fell thought that occupied him all the way home.

Artos could not read the book without help, he knew it at once. The sentences were much too long and interspersed with Latin and other languages. Perhaps that was the between the lines the dragon had meant. The only help available was Old Linn, and he did not appear until well after dinner. Unfortunately, that was the time that Artos was the busiest, feeding the dogs, checking the jesses on the hawks, cleaning the smithy. Father Bertram might have helped had he still been alive, though somehow Artos doubted it. The dragon's

99

book was neither Testament nor commentary, that much he *could* read, and the good father had been fierce about what he had considered proper fare. The castle bonfires had often burned texts of which he disapproved. Even Lady Marion's *Book of Hours*, which had taken four scribes the full part of a year to set down, had gone up in Father Bertram's righteous flames because Adam and Eve had no fig leaves. This Artos had on good authority, though he had never seen it himself, for Lady Marion had complained to Lady Sylvia who had tittered about it to her serving girls who passed the news along with the gravy to young Cai who had mentioned it as a joke to his friends in the cow shed when Artos, who had been napping in the haymow, overheard them.

No, the good Father Bertram would never have helped. Old Linn, though, was different. He could read four tongues well: English, Latin, Greek, and bardic runes. It was said his room was full of books. He could recite the "Conception of Pyrderi," a tale Artos loved for the sheer sound of it, and the stories about the children of Llyr and the Cauldron and the Iron House and the horse made for Bran. Or at least Linn used to be able to tell them all. Before he had been taken ill so suddenly and dramatically, his best piece had always been the "Battle of the Trees." Artos could not remember a time when dinners of great importance at the castle had not ended with Linn's declaiming of it. In fact, Lord Ector's Irish retainers called Linn *shanachie*, which, as far as Artos could tell from their garbled and endless explanations, simply meant "storyteller." But they said the word with awe when coupling it to Old Linn's name.

The problem, Artos thought, was that the old man hated him. Well, perhaps *hate* was too strong a word, but he seemed to prefer the young gentlemen of the house, not the impoverished fosterling. Linn especially lavished attention on Sir Cai who, as far as Artos was concerned, long ago let his muscles o'ertake his head. And Sir Bedvere, slack-jawed and hardhanded. And Sir Lancot, the pretty boy. Once Artos, too, had tried to curry favor with the trio of lordlings, fetching and carrying and helping them with their schoolwork. But then they all grew up, and the three grew up faster and taller and louder. And once Sir Lancot as a joke had pulled Artos's pants down around his ankles in the courtyard and the other two called out the serving maids to gawk. And that led to Mag's getting sweet on him, which was why he had grown to despise Mag and pity the boys, even though they were older and bigger and better placed than he.

Still, there was a time for putting aside such feelings, thought Artos. The getting of wisdom was surely such a time. He would need help in reading the dragon's book. None of the others, Cai or Bedvere or Lancot, could read half as well as he. They could only just make out the prayers in their psalters. Sir Ector could not read at all. So it would have to be Old Linn.

But to his despair, the apothecary could not be found after dinner. In desperation, he went to talk to the old man's best friend, the smith.

"Come now, young Art," called out Magnus Pieter as Artos approached the smith. "Did we not have words just yesterday? Something about a sword and a stone?"

Artos tried to think of a way to get the conversation around to Linn's whereabouts, but the conversation would not move at his direction. The smith willed it where he would. At last there was nothing left to do but remove the leathern bag around his neck and take out the jewel. He dropped it onto the anvil. It made a funny little pinging sound.

Magnus sucked on his lower lip and snorted through his nose. "By God, boy, and where'd you get that stone?"

To tell the truth meant getting swat for a liar. He suddenly realized it would be the same if he showed the book to Linn. So he lied. "I was left it by . . . Father Bertram," he said. "And I've . . ." The lies came slowly. He was by inclination an honest boy. He preferred silence to an untruth.

"Kept it till now, have you?" asked the smith. "Well, well, and of course you have. After all, there's not much in that village of ours to spend such a jewel on."

Artos nodded silently, thankful to have Magnus Pieter do the lying for him.

"And what would you be wanting for such a jewel?" asked the smith with the heavy-handed jocularity he always confused with cunning.

Knowing that he must play the innocent in order to get the better bargain, Artos said simply, "Why, a sword, of course."

"Of course!" Magnus Pieter laughed, hands on hips, throwing his head way back.

Since the other two smiths he had met laughed in just that way, Artos assumed it was something taught.

The smith stopped laughing and cocked his head to one side. "Well?"

"I am old enough to have a sword of my own," said Artos. "And now I can pay for a good one."

"How good?" asked the smith in his heavy manner.

Artos knelt before the anvil and the red jewel was at the level of his eyes. As if he were addressing the stone and not the smith, he chanted a bit from a song Old Linn used to sing:

And aye their swordes soe sore can byte,
Throughe help of gramarye . . .

From behind him the smith sighed. "Aye," the old man said, "and a good sword it shall be. A fine blade, a steel of power. And while I make it for you, young poet, you must think of a good name for your sword from this stone." He reached across Artos's shoulder and plucked up the jewel, holding it high over both their heads.

Artos stood slowly, never once taking his eyes from the jewel. For a moment he thought he saw dragon fire leaping and crackling there. Then he remembered the glowing coals of the forge. The stone reflected that, nothing more.

"Perhaps," he said, thinking out loud, "perhaps I shall call it Inter Linea."

The smith smiled. "Fine name, that. Makes me think of foreign climes." He pocketed the stone and began to work. Artos turned and left, for he had chores to do in the mews.

Each day that followed meant another slobbery kiss from Mag and another pot of stew. It seemed to Artos a rather messy prelude to wisdom. But after a week of it, he found the conversations with the dragon worth the mess.

The dragon spoke knowingly of other lands where men walked on their heads instead of feet. Of lands down beneath the sea where the bells rang in underwater churches with each passing wave. It taught Artos riddles and their answers, like

As round as an apple, as deep as a cup,
And all the king's horses can't pull it up,

which was a *well*, of course.

And it sang him ballads from the prickly, gorse-covered land of the Scots who ran naked and screaming into battle. And songs from the cold, icy Norsemen who prowled in their dragon ships. And love songs from the silk-and-honey lands of Araby.

And once the dragon taught him a trick with pots and jewels,

103

clanking and creaking noisily all the while, its huge foot mixing up the pots till Artos's head fair ached to know under which one lay the emerald as big as an egg. And that game he had used later with Lancot and Bedvere and Cai and won from them a number of gold coins till they threatened him. With his promised new sword he might have beaten them, but not with his bare hands. So he used a small man's wiles to trick them once again, picked up the winnings, and left them grumbling over the cups and peas he had used for the game.

And so day by day, week by week, month by month, Artos gained wisdom.

It took three tries and seven months before Artos had his sword. Each new steel had something unacceptable about it. The first had a hilt that did not sit comfortably in his hand. Bedvere claimed it instead, and Magnus Pieter was so pleased with the coins Sir Bedvere paid it was weeks before he was ready to work another. Instead he shoed horses, made latches, and built a gigantic candelabrum for the dining room to Lady Marion's specifications.

The second sword had a strange crossbar that the smith swore would help protect the hand. Artos thought the sword unbalanced but Cai, who prized newness over all things, insisted that he wanted that blade. Again Magnus Pieter was pleased enough to spend the weeks following making farm implements like plowshares and hoes.

The third sword was still bright with its tempering when Lancot claimed it.

"Cai and Bedvere have new swords," Lancot said, his handsome face drawn down with longing. He reached his hand out.

Artos, who had been standing in the shadows of the smithy, was about to say something when Old Linn hobbled in. His mouth and hair spoke of a lingering illness, both being yellowed and lifeless. But his voice was strong.

"You were always a man true to his word," he reminded the smith.

"And true to my swords," said Magnus Pieter, pleased with the play.

Artos stepped from the shadows then and held out his hand. The smith put the sword in it and Artos turned it this way and that to catch the light. The watering on the blade made a strange pattern that looked like the flame from a dragon's mouth. It sat well and balanced in his hand.

"He likes the blade," said Old Linn.

Magnus Pieter shrugged, smiling.

Artos turned to thank the apothecary but he was gone and so was Lancot. When he peered out the smithy door, there were the two of them walking arm in arm up the winding path toward the castle.

"So you've got your Inter Linea now," said the smith. "And about time you took one. Nothing wrong with the other two."

"*And* you got a fine price for them," Artos said.

The smith returned to his anvil, and the clang of hammer on new steel ended their conversation.

Artos ran out of the castle grounds, hallooing so loudly even the tortoise dozing on the rusted helm lifted its sleepy head. He fairly leaped over the two rocks in the path. They seemed to have gotten smaller with each trip to the dragon's lair. He was calling still when he approached the entrance to the cave.

"Ho, old flametongue," he cried out, the sword allowing him his first attempt at familiarity. "Furnace-lung, look what I have. My sword. From the stone you gave me. It is a rare beauty."

There was no answer.

Suddenly afraid that he had overstepped the bounds and that the dragon lay sulking within, Artos peered inside.

The cave was dark, cold, silent.

Slowly Artos walked in and stopped about halfway. He felt surrounded by the icy silence. But that was all. There was no sense of dragon there. No presence.

"Sir? Father dragon? Are you home?" He put a hand up to one of the hanging stones to steady himself. In the complete dark he had little sense of what was up and what was down.

Then he laughed. "Oh, I know, you have gone out on a flight." It was the only answer that came to him, though the dragon had never once mentioned flying. But everyone knows dragons have wings. And wings mean flight. Artos laughed again, a hollow little chuckle. Then he turned toward the small light of the cave entrance. "I'll come back tomorrow. At my regular time," he called over his shoulder. He said it out loud just in case the dragon's magic extended to retrieving words left in the still cave air. "Tomorrow," Artos promised.

But the pattern had been altered subtly and, like a weaving gone awry, could not be changed back to the way it had been without a weakness in the cloth.

The next day Artos did not go to the cave. Instead he practiced swordplay with willow wands in the main courtyard, beating Cai soundly and being beaten in turn by both Bedvere and Lancot.

The following morn, he and the three older boys were sent by Lady Marion on a fortnight's journey to gather gifts of jewels and silks from the market towns for the coming holy days. Some at Ector's castle celebrated the solstice with the druids, some kept the holy day for the Christ child's birth, and a few of the old soldiers still drank bull's blood and spoke of Mithras in secret meetings under the castle, for there was a vast warren of halls and rooms there. But they all gave gifts to one another at the year's turning, whichever gods they knelt to.

It was Artos's first such trip. The other boys had gone the year before under Linn's guidance. This year the four of them were given leave to go alone. Cai was so pleased he forgave Artos for the beating. Suddenly, they were the best of friends. And Bedvere and Lancot, who had beaten him, loved Artos now as well, for even when he had been on the ground with the wand at his throat and his face and arms red from the lashings, he had not cried "Hold." There had been not even the hint of tears in his eyes. They admired him for that.

With his bright new sword belted at his side, brand-new leggings from the castle stores, and the new-sworn friends riding next to him, it was no wonder Artos forgot the dragon and the dark cave. Or, if he did not exactly forget, what he remembered was that the dragon hadn't been there when he wanted it the most. So, for a few days, for a fortnight, Artos felt he could, like Cai, glory in the new.

He did not glory in the dragon. It was old, old past counting the years, old past helping him, old and forgetful.

They came home with red rosy cheeks polished by the winter wind and bags packed with treasure. An extra two horses carried the overflow.

Cai, who had lain with his first girl, a serving wench of little beauty and great reputation, was full of new boasts. Bedvere and Lancot had won a junior tourney for boys under sixteen, Bedvere with his sword and Lancot his lance. And though Artos had been a favorite on the outbound trip, full of wonderful stories, riddles, and songs, as they turned toward home he had lapsed into long silences. By the time they were but a day's hard ride away, it was as if his mouth were bewitched.

The boys teased him, thinking it was Mag who worried him.

"Afraid of Old Garlic, then?" asked Cai. "At least Rosemary's breath was sweet." (Rosemary being the serving wench's name.)

"Or are you afraid of my sword?" said Bedvere.

"Or my lance?" Lancot added brightly.

When he kept silent, they tried to wheedle the cause of his set lips by reciting castle gossip. Every maiden, every alewife, every false nurse was named. Then they turned their attention to the men. They never mentioned dragons, though, for they did not know one lived by the castle walls. Artos had never told them of it.

But it was the dragon, of course, that concerned him. With each mile he remembered the darkness, the complete silence of the cave. At night he dreamed of it, the cave opening staring down from the hill like the empty eye socket of a long-dead beast.

They unpacked the presents carefully and carried them up to Lady Marion's quarters. She, in turn, fed them wine and cakes in her apartments, a rare treat. Her minstrel, a handsome boy except for his wandering left eye, sang a number of songs while they ate, even one in a Norman dialect. Artos drank only a single mouthful of the sweet wine. He ate nothing. He had heard all the songs before.

Thus it was well past sundown before Lady Marion let them go.

Artos would not join the others who were going to report to Lord Ector. He pushed past Cai and ran down the stairs. The other boys called after him, but he ignored them. Only the startled ends of their voices followed him.

He hammered on the gate until the guards lifted the iron portcullis, then he ran across the moat bridge. Dark muddy lumps in the mushy ice were the only signs of life.

As he ran, he held his hand over his heart, cradling the two pieces of cake he had slipped into his tunic. Since he had had no time to beg stew from Mag, he hoped seed cakes would do instead. He did not, for a moment, believe the dragon had starved to death without his poor offering of stew. The dragon had existed many years before

109

Artos had found the cave. It was not the *size* of the stew, but the *fact* of it.

He stubbed his toe on the second outcropping hard enough to force a small mewing sound between his lips. The tor was icy and that made climbing it difficult. Foolishly he'd forgotten his gloves with his saddle gear. And he'd neglected to bring a light.

When he got to the mouth of the cave and stepped in, he was relieved to hear heavy breathing echoing off the cave wall, until he realized it was the sound of his own ragged breath.

"Dragon!" he cried out, his voice a misery.

Suddenly there was a small moan and an even smaller glow, like dying embers that have been breathed upon one last time.

"Is that you, my son?" The voice was scarcely a whisper, so quiet the walls could not find enough to echo.

"Yes, dragon," said Artos. "It is I."

"Did you bring me any stew?"

"Only two seed cakes."

"I like seed cakes."

"Then I'll bring them to you."

"Noooooooo." The sound held only the faintest memory of the powerful voice of before.

But Artos had already started toward the back of the cave, one hand in front to guide himself around the overhanging rocks. He was halfway there when he stumbled against something and fell heavily to his knees. Feeling around, he touched a long, metallic curved blade.

"Has someone been here? Has someone tried to slay you?" he cried. Then, before the dragon could answer, Artos's hand traveled farther along the blade to its strange metallic base.

His hands told him what his eyes could not; his mouth spoke what his heart did not want to hear. "It is the dragon's foot."

He leaped over the metal construct and scrambled over a small rocky wall. Behind it, in the dying glow of a small fire, lay an old man on a straw bed. Near him were tables containing beakers full of colored liquids—amber, rose, green, and gold. On the wall were strange toothed wheels with handles.

The old man raised himself on one arm. "Pendragon," he said and tried to set his lips into a welcoming smile. "Son."

"Old Linn," replied Artos angrily, "I am no son of yours."

"There was once," the old man began quickly, settling into a story before Artos's anger had time to gel, "a man who would know Truth. And he traveled all over the land looking."

Without willing it, Artos was pulled into the tale.

"He looked along the seacoasts and in the quiet farm dales. He went into the country of lakes and across vast deserts seeking Truth. At last, one dark night in a small cave atop a hill, he found her. Truth was a wizened old woman with but a single tooth left in her head. Her eyes were rheumy. Her hair greasy strands. But when she called him into her cave, her voice was low and lyric and pure and that was how he knew he had found Truth."

Artos stirred uneasily.

The old man went on. "He stayed a year and a day by her side and learned all she had to teach. And when his time was done, he said, 'My Lady Truth, I must go back to my own home now. But I would do something for you in exchange.'" Linn stopped. The silence between them grew until it was almost a wall.

"Well, what did she say?" Artos asked at last.

"She told him, 'When you speak of me, tell your people that I am young and beautiful.'"

For a moment Artos said nothing. Then he barked out a short, quick laugh. "So much for Truth."

111

Linn sat up and patted the mattress beside him, an invitation that Artos ignored. "Would you have listened these seven months to an old apothecary who had a tendency to fits?"

"You did not tell me the truth."

"I did not lie. You *are* the dragon's son."

Artos set his mouth and turned his back on the old man. His voice came out low and strained. *"I . . . am . . . not . . . your . . . son."*

"It is true that you did not spring from my loins," said the old man. "But I carried you here to Ector's castle and waited and hoped you would seek out my wisdom. But you longed for the truth of lance and sword. I did not have that to give." His voice was weak and seemed to end in a terrible sigh.

Artos did not turn around. "I believed in the dragon."

Linn did not answer.

"I *loved* the dragon."

The silence behind him was so loud that at last Artos turned around. The old man had fallen onto his side and lay still. Artos felt something warm on his cheeks and realized it was tears. He ran to Linn and knelt down, pulling the old man onto his lap. As he cradled him, Linn opened his eyes.

"Did you bring me any stew?" he asked.

"I . . ." The tears were falling unchecked now. "I brought you seed cakes."

"I like seed cakes," Linn said. "But couldn't you get any stew from Old Garlic?"

Artos felt his mouth drop open. "How did you know about her?"

The old man smiled, showing terrible teeth. He whispered, "I am the Great Riddler. I am the Master of Wisdoms. I am the Word and I am the Light. I Was and Am and Will Be." He hesitated. "I am The Dragon."

Artos smiled back and then carefully stood with the old man in his arms. He was amazed at how frail Linn was. His bones, Artos thought, must be as hollow as the wing bones of a bird.

There was a door in the cave wall and Linn signaled him toward it. Carrying the old apothecary through the doorway, Artos marveled at the runes carved in the lintel. Past the door was a warren of hallways and rooms. From somewhere ahead he could hear the chanting of many men.

Artos looked down at the old man and whispered to him. "Yes. I understand. You *are* the dragon, indeed. And I am the dragon's boy. But I will not let you die just yet. I have not finished getting my wisdom."

Smiling broadly, the old man turned toward him like a baby rooting at its mother's breast, found the seed cakes, ate one of them and then, with a gesture both imperious and fond, stuffed the other in Artos's mouth.

The University of Massachusetts, where my husband is a professor, is near our home. One year the science fiction club asked me to come to its annual convention and give a speech. My speech was about the making of dragons from the writer's point of view, and I ended with this comic poem.

Of course, I love to see my writing in print and so as soon as the conference was over, I sent the poem to Isaac Asimov's Science Fiction Magazine. The magazine took it, paid me for it, and eventually printed it on two pages. (Just as well; I had spoken for free to the UMass SF Club!)

A year after the poem was published, my oldest son—who is a rock-and-roll musician—got a tattoo, something he knew I would hate. But the tattoo was the illustration used in the magazine for this poem. How could I be entirely angry with him?

The Making of Dragons

If only it were still simple,
fire, water, earth, air,
                            the staples
of the older gods. But modern days
require choice, that modern phrase.
So choose—good dragon, bad dragon, west or east.
We must prioritize your beast.
You buy your myth with hollow coins.
So choose:
                fire in the mouth or in the loins.

The Head:
                the placement of the jagged teeth,
the poison glands, above, beneath
the forking tongue.

Eyes that spark fire?
The mouth, when open, breathing desire?
The jaw reticulated, viz. the snake.
The voice articulated, viz. the crake.
The tone: a cry, a scream, a roar?
In the making of dragons less is not more.

The Trunk:
the body comes in three basic styles.
One, the sinuous body that goes on for miles
(or metres in our continental design).
That is our Ororoborus line.
Two, the stumpy, humpy dinosaur
which will cost you a bit more
but comes with guarantees in parts replacement.
(We keep a year's supply in our basement.)
The third, imported from the east,
well, we recommend that one the least.

The Tail:
caudal vertebrae aside,
a tail can be narrow or it can be wide,
it can be flexible or it can be hard,
used for a rudder, a weapon, a guard,
but all tails must be a certain length
to guarantee balance, poise, and strength.
Here is the formula (or as we say in the trade, the key):

Length from nose to sacrum $+ 2 \times 2\frac{1}{2}$ equals tail
or
$$NSL + 2 \times 2.5 = T$$

Options:
        scales, feathers, skin, or fur.
Sexes: him, it, hermaphro, her.
Nails: oak, teak, ivory, or steel.
Diet preferences: beef, chicken, pork, game, or veal,
vegetarian (this last within reason),
or maidens in or out of season.

Our payment plan is based on need.
We take your house, your soul, your seed.
Please understand:
        a dragon is a work of art.
If you prefer installments, we take your heart.
Just initial your preferred design
and here, on the bottom line . . .
        sign.

I had always wanted to write a Chinese dragon story because Chinese dragons are so different from the Western variety. Unlike their Western counterparts, Chinese dragons are rain spirits and though they are fierce and unpredictable, they can be helpful to humans whose good hearts they admire.

When I began this story, it was a very short story called "The Pocket Beast" and was not about dragons at all. But as I read several Chinese folklore books (notably Hackin's Asiatic Mythology and Eberhard's Folktales of China), I fell in love with the dragon kings and the wang-liang trolls with their gifts. The hero One Ox suddenly developed brothers and a mother. I scribbled notes to myself on a bus ride into New York City, lost the notes, and when I returned home, wrote an entirely different story from the one I had planned.

This story took about a year, from start to finish, and made several devious turnings along the way. I hadn't expected there to be three dragon kings, for example. Nor had I known that Three Ox was going to be the real hero.

It must be noted, however, that though I have used many elements from Chinese mythology—the pocket beast, the wang-liang's face, the silver hairpin, the names of all the dragon kings—this is not a Chinese story. The solution to the Ox brothers' problem is entirely Western and influenced by the many fairy tales from European sources that I have read over the years.

One Ox, Two Ox, Three Ox, and the Dragon King

There was once a poor farmer who had but a small farm and no beasts to help him plow. When his wife gave birth to a son, the farmer insisted on calling the boy One Ox. "For," the farmer said, "someday he will work with me in the field."

118

When his wife gave birth a year later to a second son, the boy was called Two Ox.

And a year after that, their third son was named Three Ox.

But before the boys were old enough to help, the farmer died, leaving the poor farm to his wife. She worked hard and the farm managed to support the four of them, but barely. And when the boys were big enough, they worked harder still.

Each evening after toiling all day in the fields, the boys would sit by the fire eating their rice and drinking their tea. To make them laugh and to teach them of the great wide world, their mother would tell them stories. Some of the stories were of wizards and some of the stories were of warriors; some of the stories were of kinship and some of the stories were of kings. But at the end of each tale, she would sigh and say, "Alas that all I have to give to you, my sons, are these tales. The farm is so small and so poor, it cannot be shared. Only one of you can inherit it when I die."

"Which one?" they would ask every night.

But each night her answer was the same: "Whoever works the hardest."

"And the one who works the hardest—that one you love the best?" they would ask.

"How can I choose between my dear sons?" she always answered. "I love you each the best." And with that answer, they had to be content.

Now one year the farmer's wife caught a chill, grew sick, and all but died. The boys went without rice in order to pay for a doctor. But after he examined her, the old potion-maker shook his head. "Nothing in the world can save her."

"If nothing *in* the world can save her," said One Ox, "then is there something *out* of it?"

"Name it and we will find it," said Two Ox.

"Though we must go to the ends of the earth," added Three Ox. "For just so much do we love our mother."

"Only the Waters of Life can save her now," the doctor said.

"And where can the waters be found?" the three boys asked together.

"In the cave of the Dragon King," the old man answered, packing up his potions and pins, "is a ring of power. Put that ring in a glass of clear water, and when it is drunk, the sick are made well."

"Where is this cave?" asked One Ox.

"And who is the Dragon King?" asked Two Ox.

Three Ox was silent.

"As to the cave," the old doctor said, "it is beyond the farthest mountains and then one mountain farther. And as to the Dragon King, I would not want to meet him myself. His name is Lung-Wang, and he is said to be more than a *li* in length—five hundred yards. He has horns on top of his head, and he is covered with scales. It is bad enough to meet one of the lesser kings, the Nagas. Do not seek out Lung-Wang if you value your lives."

Only then did Three Ox speak. "Our mother's life *is* our lives, and you have said only the Waters of Life will save her."

The doctor pulled his long beard and looked both sad and wise. "That is merely a way of saying that she is beyond help, my son."

"Nevertheless," said Three Ox, "we will help her. We could do nothing for our father when he died for we were too young. But now we are older and stronger. We will find these waters or die."

"Then," the doctor said solemnly, "you may very well die. Lung-Wang will not give up the Waters of Life, his most precious gift, just for the asking. He will demand three magical objects in trade. To get one is difficult; to get two is nearly impossible; to get three is beyond belief."

One Ox looked sad.

Two Ox looked puzzled.

"Nevertheless," said Three Ox, "it will be done." And his brothers nodded quickly. They commended their mother to the doctor's good care and set out within the hour.

Following the sun, the boys walked toward the nearest mountains. Each had but a single coin in his pocket; the rest of the family's small savings had been left to pay the doctor's fee.

They had not been gone but an hour past noon when One Ox turned to his brothers.

"The doctor has said we need three magical objects to trade, but he did not say which three, nor where they might be found. Perhaps we should separate and each search for one. That way our chances will be tripled. We could meet back here in seven days."

Two Ox nodded. "A fine plan, my brother, but for this one thing: our dear mother is much too weak to last that long. I propose we meet back in five days."

Three Ox likewise nodded, adding, "There is, of course, still the Dragon King's cave to find. Perhaps we should meet back here in three days, not five, else our dear mother will be in her grave and all the Waters of Life will not save her then."

So they agreed on three, and at a triple fork in the road, One Ox went east, Two Ox went west, and Three Ox went forward toward the nearest hills. They did not even take the time to wave good-bye.

To the east were the high towers of the city of Kai-lung. It was the city in which the Master of Masters, the magician Kuang-li, lived. It was said of her that if she called a man blind, that man would become blind in an instant; if she called him emperor, he would be crowned within the week.

One Ox walked toward Kai-lung until his feet ached and his stomach proclaimed its emptiness, but he did not dare rest. He thought only of his sick mother and the magic gift he might find within the city walls.

It was near dark when he reached Kai-lung and full night before he found a place to sleep in a narrow niche within a wall. "In the morning," he told himself, "I will seek out a magician and see if I can beg a gift of him."

The morning dawned early and One Ox looked out from the niche, seeing for the first time how a city stirs in the light. Carters pulled and pushed their creaking wagons; vendors began to call out their wares; and a little flower girl, no more than five years old, stood below the window of the tallest of the tall towers crying up, "Peonies for the Master of Masters. Flowers for the Dragon of Kai-lung."

A hand with nails as long as knives extended out of the tower window and lowered a willow basket on a rope. When the basket settled on the ground, the child knelt down, extracted a single coin from it, and placed a bunch of flowers in the coin's stead. Then she pulled three times on the rope. Slowly the long-nailed hand drew up the rope and basket to the window and, with a wink, rope, basket, and all were gone.

One Ox stood and brushed his dark hair back with his hands. Going over to the child, he asked, "Who is this Master of Masters? Who is this Dragon of Kai-lung?"

The girl looked surprised. "Everyone knows that."

"I am not everyone," said One Ox. "And I assure you that I do not know."

The child looked guilelessly into his eyes. "Kuang-li is one of the Nagas, a dragon master of the highest degree. If Kuang-li calls you by your true name, you will belong to the Master forever."

"Then I shall not say my name," said One Ox, "for I have no time to remain in this city for more than a single day and surely not forever. But I *would* like to purchase a piece of this Master's magic."

"Then," the child said before turning away, "you will have to get into the tower, though it has no stairs, for Kuang-li does not come out during the day, and at night in dragon form flies over our city, guarding it from the dangers of the dark."

One Ox thought long and hard about this, and by evening he had an idea. With his single coin, he purchased a bunch of flowers from another flower seller. Then, just before the sun went down, he stood directly under the tower so that he could not be seen from above, and cried out in imitation of the child, "Peonies for the Master of Masters. Flowers for the Dragon of Kai-lung."

For a long moment he waited, wondering if his coin had been spent in vain. But at last the hand with the long nails extended out of the tower window, lowering the willow basket. One Ox did not take time even to extract the coin inside. Instead, placing the flowers in the basket, he grabbed hold of the rope and quickly, hand over hand, climbed up the tower wall. Once at the window, he flung himself over the sill.

"You look little like a peony, my eager friend," said a voice as old and cracked as leather.

When One Ox looked up, there was a serving woman whose face was as lined as a map, but whether amusement or condemnation were written there, he could not tell. She turned from him and brought up the basket, then took the flowers out and placed them in a blue-glazed jar.

Only when she was done did she turn to him again. "Come, speak quickly, tell me what you want."

"Old mother, I wish to speak to your master, the Master of Masters," One Ox said. "I wish to speak to Kuang-li."

"Are you not afraid of the dragon?" asked the old woman.

"My need is greater than my fear," said One Ox.

"And your ignorance exceeds them both," said the old woman. "But I will forgive you this once."

One Ox stood, towering over the old woman. "I ask you again, mother of mothers, take me to Kuang-li."

"And I will forgive you twice," said the old woman. "But not once more. Do you speak to all mothers this way?"

Suddenly remembering his manners, One Ox bowed his head. "Forgive me, but it is because my own mother lies sick that I must see the Dragon of Kai-lung."

"Then listen well, son of a dying mother, *I* am the Master of Masters. *I* am the Dragon of Kai-lung. And when the sun goes down and I become the Naga in truth, I will be much tempted by the meat in your young arms and thighs still warm from the heat of the sun." She reached out with her long nails and pinched his arm as she spoke.

One Ox shivered. "O mighty dragon," he began, terrified at how badly he had started and not at all sure there was any way to change what had begun. "The doctor says that my mother is beyond all help save that of the Waters of Life. But we cannot get the waters without three magical objects in exchange. My brothers and I have each gone out on the road to find such pieces of magic to trade with the Dragon King."

"And you thought . . ." the old woman said, turning her head to look out of the window, where the sun was fast fading behind the hills, "that I would give you such a thing."

"I was hoping . . ." One Ox said, his head bowed low.

"And what will you give *me*?" she asked, her voice beginning to roughen. When One Ox dared to look up, he saw she had sprouted a horn on each side of her head.

"I have . . . I have only myself," he said, looking down again quickly. "But you may have that if it will save my mother. I will give you myself—and my name. I am called One Ox."

"Good answer," the old woman said. "I will not eat you now." Only this time, her tongue stuck out as she spoke, and it was red and forked. She reached into her pocket and pulled out a tiny folded packet, not quite paper and not quite skin. "When you get to the ground unfold this. It is a bit of magic that even the Dragon King will envy. And when your mother is well again, come back to Kai-lung." She handed him the packet. "I will work you hard for a year."

"I am not afraid of hard work," One Ox said, his eyes on the ground.

"But be afraid of me," came the response.

When One Ox looked up, a dragon the blue-black of midnight stood before him.

"Be very afraid." Its silver teeth glittered like stars in that night sky.

One Ox's knees trembled and there was a bitter taste in his mouth. As he watched, the dragon shook out its great blue-black wings, arched its back, and ran its claws along the floor. The claws drew runnels like rivers in the wood. Then the dragon leaped through the tower window and was gone.

One Ox drew in a long breath, and by the time he had let it out again, the full moon had risen over the hills. He could see the silhouette of the dragon as it sailed across the sky, as clean and crisp as if cut from paper.

"The dragon will not return until morning," One Ox thought. "I should leave at once." But when he looked around the tower room, his old habits claimed him. He found a broom and swept away the petals from the peonies that had fallen in the rush of air from the dragon's wings. He washed out a teacup. He straightened the dragon's

125

bed. What with one thing and another, he was not finished in the tower until almost dawn and so tired he lay down on the floor and fell fast asleep. He did not see the dragon return, nor did he see it change back into the old woman. He woke only when she touched his arm.

"Come, my good worker, come," she said. "You have pleased me well. But now you must go. Your brothers will be waiting." And she held the rope for him so that he might reach the ground in safety.

No sooner did his feet touch the street than the Master of Masters pulled up the rope and basket and they disappeared in a wink.

One Ox took the packet from his pocket. It weighed hardly an ounce. Slowly he began to unfold it, one piece at a time. He was halfway through the unfolding before he realized it was a tiny pony made of cloth as brown as earth, with a foam-colored mane and tail. When the last fold lay flat in his hand, the pony gave a high-pitched whinny. This so startled One Ox that he dropped it to the ground.

The minute it touched the ground, the tiny pony began to grow. Bigger and bigger it grew until it was the size of a large horse. One Ox put his hand on its back, and the horse turned its head toward him. Its eyes were like black gems with a red fire at each center.

Though he had never ridden a horse before, One Ox had seen men ride by the farm, and he knew just what to do. Leaping onto its back, he threaded his fingers into its foam-colored mane. The horse reared once, then raced down the road, swift as the east wind, to the place of the three forks.

In the meanwhile, Two Ox had gone west, and to the west was the sea, down in whose depths lived the Master of Masters, the wizard Kuang-jun. It was said of Kuang-jun that if he called a man old, that man would wither as the words were spoken; and if he called a man living, even a corpse would kick up its heels.

Two Ox walked toward the Western Sea until his feet ached and his stomach proclaimed its emptiness, but he did not dare rest. He thought only of his sick mother and the magic gift he might find on the banks of the sea.

It was near dark when he reached the shore, and he stood a long time watching the waves as they stretched and flattened upon the sand. He saw no one near and no one far away, so he lay down and slept on a gray rock.

The morning dawned early and Two Ox looked up from the rock, seeing for the first time how a beach stirs in the morning's light. Crabs scuttled across the sand; gulls dived down to pick them up; and a little fisher lad, no more than five years old, threw an orange net filled with gray stones into the sea, crying, "Silver coins for silver cockles, O Master of Masters. Silver coins for silver fish, O Dragon of the Western Sea." When he drew in his net, it was filled with cockleshells and tiny fish leaping up as if on the boil. But of the silver stones there was no sign.

Two Ox stood up and smoothed down his shirt and pants. Going over to the child, he asked, "Who is this Master of Masters? Who is the Dragon of the Western Sea?"

The boy looked surprised. "Everyone knows that."

"I am not everyone," said Two Ox. "And I assure you I do not know."

The boy looked innocently into Two Ox's eyes. "Kuang-jun is one of the Nagas, a dragon master of the highest degree. If Kuang-jun calls you by your true name, you will belong to the master forever."

"Then I shall not say my name," said Two Ox, "for I do not have time to remain by the sea for more than this one day, and surely not forever. But I *would* like to purchase a piece of this master's magic."

The child spread out his net to dry in the sun. "Then you will have to throw yourself into the water and learn to breathe it, for

Kuang-jun lives beneath the waves. Except at night, when he flies in dragon form up and down the western shore, he does not come up out of the sea."

Two Ox thought long and hard about this. At last he said to the child, "I have but a single coin. If you would give me the loan of your net for the rest of this day and this night, I will give the coin to you. Tomorrow, whatever my fate, you will have your net back."

The child nodded solemnly, took the coin, picked up his fish basket, and went away.

Two Ox contemplated the ocean all that afternoon, but at last he knew there was no other way. Wrapping himself in the net, with silver beach stones for weights, he waded out into the ocean. The water was cold and final around his legs.

Then, in imitation of the child, he cried out, "Silver coins for silver cockles, O Master of Masters. Silver coins for silver fish, O Dragon of the Western Sea." His voice seemed to sink down, down, down into the dark water and he flung himself after it.

The waves tumbled him over and over, stripping away the netting and his shirt and trousers and shoes. It scoured his skin and the shells of his ears, it rubbed away and scrubbed away all thoughts of the shore. And when it was done with him, it dumped him down upon a broad white road underneath the sea. He took a deep breath and, surprised to find it was air, opened his eyes. At the end of the road was a castle made of shells. He pushed his way through the water toward it and, upon entering, found himself face to face with an old, old serving man in a bright red robe. The man's face was the color of weak tea, and his shoulders were bowed with age.

"Old man," Two Ox began, the words as round as bubbles, "I wish to speak to your master, the Master of Masters. I wish to speak to Kuang-jun."

"Are you not afraid of the dragon?" asked the old man.

129

"My need is greater than my fear," said Two Ox.

"And your foolishness exceeds them both," said the old man. "But I will forgive you this once."

Two Ox drew himself up. He towered over the old man. "Do not confuse my nakedness with unpreparedness, old father. Take me to this Kuang-jun."

"And I will forgive your bad manners twice," said the old man. He handed Two Ox a ceremonial robe the color of the sea.

Suddenly ashamed of his behavior, Two Ox put on the robe and bowed his head. "Forgive me, but it is because my mother lies ill and would have died already to see me in such fashion. It is for her sake that I must see the Dragon of the Western Sea."

"Then listen well, son of a dying mother: *I* am the Master of Masters. *I* am the Dragon of the Western Sea. And when the sun goes down, darkening even these dark waters, I become the Naga in truth. Then I will be much tempted by the meat in your arms and thighs, now salted to my taste by the waves." He reached out and pinched Two Ox on the arm.

Two Ox shivered, though the robe was warm. "O mighty dragon," he began, "the doctor says that my mother is beyond all help save that of the Waters of Life. But to get the waters my brothers and I need three magical objects to trade. We have each gone out on the road to find such pieces of magic to tempt the Dragon King."

The old man smiled, looking up toward the top of the waves which were, even then, beginning to darken. When he looked down again, bubbles formed around his head like horns. "And you thought I would just *give* you such a thing."

"I was hoping beyond hope . . ." Two Ox said, his head bowed low.

"And what will you give me in exchange?" the old man asked.

His voice grew rough, and when Two Ox looked again he saw that green scales were beginning to form on the old man's face.

"I had but a single coin," Two Ox said, "with which I purchased the use of the net. And my clothes were all stripped away by the waves. All I have left to give you is myself"—he hesitated for a moment—"and my name." He took a deep breath and tasted salt in his mouth. "I am called Two Ox."

"Good answer," the old man said. "I will not eat you now." But when he spoke, his tongue stuck out and it was black and forked. He reached into the pocket of his robe and pulled out a silver hairpin. "When you are once again on land," he said, "use this when need is great. This is a piece of magic even the Dragon King will envy. And when your mother is once again well, come back to the Western Sea." He handed the hairpin to Two Ox. "I will work you hard for a year."

"I am not afraid of hard work," Two Ox said.

"But be very afraid of me," came the response. And as Two Ox watched, the old man changed completely into a dragon the green-black of the sea, its silver teeth glittering like the tops of waves.

Two Ox's knees trembled, and he let out a soft moan. As he watched, the green-black dragon shook out its great green-black wings, lashed its mighty tail like a rudder, and sailed off through the water in a cascade of foam.

When the bubbles at last subsided, Two Ox thought to himself, "The dragon will not return until morning. I should leave at once." But when he looked around the shell castle, he saw that everything had been greatly disturbed by the dragon's leaving, and his old land habits claimed him. He picked up the bright red robe and hung it on a peg. He straightened the matting on the floor. He tidied up the dishes. And what with one thing and another, he was not done in

131

the sea castle until the first waves of light had filtered down from above. And then he was so tired, he fell asleep on the floor and so did not see the dragon return, nor see it change back into the old man. He woke only when he was shaken.

"Come, my good worker, come," the old man said. "You have already pleased me well. But now you must go. Your brothers will be waiting." He took Two Ox's ceremonial robe and handed him trousers, shirt, shoes, and the child's netting. Then he gave Two Ox a push that was so hard, Two Ox was propelled straight through the water and onto the shore.

No sooner did Two Ox's feet touch the beach than he got dressed. He found the hairpin stuck into the waistband of his trousers. Spreading the fisher lad's netting out to dry, Two Ox removed the hairpin and looked at it. It caught the sunlight and shimmered. When he touched the tip, it pricked his finger and he cried out, dropping the pin to the sand. No sooner did it touch the sand than a fountain of water sprang up.

Two Ox bent down, picked up the pin by the head, and drew its point along the sand. A river of silver water tumbled into the groove, and a silver boat bounced up and down on the waves. Two Ox climbed into the boat and, using the hairpin as a rudder, steered himself down the stream toward the road and the three forks.

Meanwhile, Three Ox had gone forward into the hills. There were no Nagas in the hills, only spirits like elves and ghosts and— worst of all—the *wang-liang*, ogres whose bodies are covered with coarse hair and who devour any human being whole.

Three Ox walked into the hills until his feet ached and his stomach proclaimed its emptiness, but he did not dare rest. He thought only of his sick mother and the magic gift he might find somewhere in the hills.

But as the way grew steeper and darker, Three Ox decided to cut himself a stick—pointed at one end, it would help him with the walking; pointed at the other, it could serve as a weapon.

No sooner had he done this than he heard a noise and, turning, saw a strange creature following him. Head to foot it was covered with coarse orange-brown hair, and when it smiled its teeth were sharp and long.

"Who are you?" Three Ox asked.

"Give me a coin and you may pass," the creature said.

"I have already passed," said Three Ox.

"Give me a coin and I shall not eat you," said the creature.

"I will not make much of a meal," said Three Ox.

"Give me a coin," said the creature, "and my magic is yours."

Three Ox dug into his pocket and pulled out the single coin. He tossed it to the ogre. The ogre bit into the coin, swallowed it, and laughed.

"I lied!" the ogre cried. "You will still be mine." It leaped.

Three Ox held the stick in front of him, one point at his own breast, one at the ogre, for he thought, "If the ogre is to eat me, at least I will not be alive to suffer it." But unaccountably the ogre hesitated in the air, as if held there by invisible ties.

"O mortal," the ogre screamed, "how did you know only such a pointed stick at your breast and mine would stop me?"

Three Ox hadn't known, but he thought he should not tell that to the ogre. "Everyone knows such tricks," he said.

"O mortal," the monster cried, "let me go and I promise I will not harm you."

Three Ox thought to himself that such a promise was bought too cheaply. "What more will you give me?"

"I will give you back your coin," the ogre cried.

"That's one," Three Ox said.

"I will give you my boot," said the ogre. "Have you not heard of such boots? They can run many miles." The ogre smiled.

Three Ox did not like the ogre's smile nor the way the coarse hair blew in and out of its mouth as it spoke. Then he remembered an old story his mother had told.

"The boot you offer me is a coffin. If I take it from you, I will lie in it forever."

The ogre gnashed its teeth and spoke curses that blued the air. "Then will you take my hat?"

Three Ox did not like the eager way the ogre spoke, nor that the nails on the hands offering the hat were the color of a storm-stirred pond. He remembered another story his mother had told.

"The hat you offer me is a funeral fire," he said. "If I take it I will be burned to ashes."

The *wang-liang* gnashed its awful teeth and roared until the grass wilted in three circles around it. "Then what will you have?"

Three Ox smiled. He remembered still another story his mother had recited. "I will have my coin," he said. Then while the monster spit up the money, he added, "And I will have your face!"

The *wang-liang* screamed until the trees near them shivered and lost their bark, but Three Ox was not moved. And so the ogre had to strip the very skin from its face with its muddy brown nails.

"Remember your promise," said Three Ox, slipping the face into his pocket. Then he set down the pointed stick.

The *wang-liang* whimpered, and holding its hands in front of its blank face, wandered away into the forest leaving a trail of ashes wherever it stepped.

Three Ox found a cozy cave in which to shelter for the night and in the morning headed back down the way he had come.

As Three Ox had a full day on his brothers, he arrived at the place of the three forks first. There he sat down with his back to a tree, and flipping the coin, thought about the ogre's face in his pocket. His mother's story had said such a face made the wearer invisible.

"But the *wang-liang* himself wore the face, and he could be seen," he reminded himself. It was a puzzle. Still it was worth trying. So he pulled the face from his pocket and drew it over his head.

He looked down at his hands. They were no longer there.

He looked down at his feet. *They* were no longer there.

He picked up a leaf. It disappeared.

He touched the tree. Where his fingers met the bark, the bark disappeared. But the rest—branch and root and buds and leaves—was there to see.

Smiling, he drew off the face and put it back into his pocket.

"Here is a piece of magic that the Dragon King will envy," he said to himself. He spent the rest of the day looking for food and feasting on berries. The night passed quickly, and in the morning of the third day he knew it was time for his brothers to arrive.

"I can surprise them," he said as he pulled the *wang-liang*'s face down over his. Invisible, he sat down and waited.

Suddenly by his invisible feet a river began to run, glittering silver in the morning light. Three Ox stared up the river and saw a silver boat bobbing along the current. Sitting in the back and steering with a silver rudder was Two Ox, smiling to himself.

The boat reached the river's end, and Two Ox got out. He took the silver rudder from its lock, and it became a silver pin. At the same moment, both boat and river disappeared. Smiling even more broadly, Two Ox stuck the pin through the waistband of his trousers and sat down to rest.

"As I am the first," he said aloud, "I must now wait; and as I had little time for sleep at the dragon's home, I will take a rest." He lay down and was soon snoring.

Invisible, Three Ox watched his brother for some time, and when he was sure nothing would wake Two Ox, he drew out the silver pin from his brother's waistband. Then he waited to see what more would happen.

Soon the sounds of horse's hooves came to his ears. And as he watched, a brown horse with a foam-colored mane and tail came galloping to the place of the three forks. Atop its back was One Ox, grinning broadly. When One Ox saw Two Ox asleep by the road-side, he dismounted and patted the horse on its flank. Then he pulled the horse's head until its nose touched its neck, pushed the horse onto its knees, and wrapped the tail up over its back. The horse gave a tiny whinny and shrank and shrank and shrank until it was the size of a folded letter. He slipped it into the pocket of his shirt.

"If my brother can sleep, so can I," One Ox whispered. "For I got little rest in the dragon's house." And he lay down by Two Ox's side. Within minutes he too was snoring.

When Three Ox was certain nothing would wake his brothers, he knelt beside them and drew out the folded horse from One Ox's pocket. Then he stood and waited to see what else would happen.

After many minutes the two brothers awoke.

"I was the first!" said Two Ox.

"Indeed you were," said One Ox. "And I the second. But where is that laggard youngest brother of ours?" For, as Three Ox still wore the *wang-liang*'s face, he was invisible. "Once he is here, I shall show you both the great piece of magic I have." One Ox tapped his pocket but there was no crackling sound. He reached into his pocket. There was nothing there. Turning on his brother, he shouted, "You have stolen my piece of magic while I slept!" He raised his fist.

"Wait, I too was asleep," said Two Ox. "And what need have I for your magic when I have magic of my own? I will show it to you." He felt along the waistband of his trousers. There was no pin. "Aieee, my brother, you have taken what is mine!" He raised his own fist.

Just then Three Ox laughed, and the brothers, hearing the sound but seeing no one, grew very afraid.

"Who is it?" they cried as one. "Who is there?" And they stood back to back, ready to defend one another.

Three Ox drew off the *wang-liang's* face and was visible at once. Stuffing the mask into his pocket, he handed the folded horse to One Ox, the silver hairpin to Two Ox. "Brothers, we must trust one another," he said, "but trust no one else. The two of you went to sleep and anyone—man or monster—could have stolen your magic. What then would our poor mother do? Come, we must take our three pieces of power and make our way to the Dragon King."

Ashamed, One Ox and Two Ox bowed their heads, for they knew Three Ox was right. And taking what was theirs, they followed their youngest brother along the road.

They went beyond the mountains and there, as the doctor had said, was one mountain farther. Neither horse nor boat could help them now, for the way was too rough for the horse, and what rivers could be made to spring up along the crags flowed downward.

Three Ox showed them how to take a stick and sharpen both ends, in case of ogres, but none came to trouble them on their climb. Indeed, the mountain was strangely still. No birds, no frogs, no bears called out. It was as if a great magic had silenced them all. Even the three brothers had trouble speaking as they climbed.

At last, after many hours of effort, they saw a cave.

"Should we go in?" asked One Ox.

"Dare we go in?" asked Two Ox.

"How can we not?" asked Three Ox, so they entered.

A cold wind seemed to blow through the cave, carrying with it a fine fragrance; something like jasmine, something like rain. A thin fragment of sound was carried in the wind as well, like the ringing of silver bells.

"This must be the cave of the Dragon King," said Three Ox.

"Be kind to old serving women," cautioned One Ox.

"Be kind to old serving men," added Two Ox.

The wind's fragrance turned to dust and ashes; the sound of the bells became a roar. One Ox and Two Ox turned to face the oncoming wind, holding their hands over their eyes. They did not see Three Ox slip the *wang-liang*'s face over his own and disappear.

"Who has dared enter the palace of the Dragon King?" came a voice out of the wind, a soft voice that was somehow more terrible than a scream.

"We are sons of a poor farmer, O Master of Masters," One Ox and Two Ox said together.

The wind swirled suddenly in the center of the cave, kicking up dirt and sticks and tiny stones which suddenly formed into the shape of a very large man. He had a long beard and mustaches drooping down either side of his mouth like twin waterfalls of hair. His gown was gray-green, like old moss, and emblazoned with dark green dragons. He did not smile.

"What do two farm boys have to do with me?" the man asked. "For I am Lung-Wang, King of all the Dragons." Though he asked a question, he did not look at them but stared at the ring on his hand, the center of which contained a shiny pearl as large as a pea.

"Two?" whispered One Ox.

"Two?" whispered Two Ox.

Then they mentioned it no more, guessing their youngest brother had some plan in mind.

139

"O mighty Lung-Wang," said One Ox bowing low, "our mother is desperately ill." He did not dare look up.

"And needs to drink of the Waters of Life," said Two Ox, bowing even lower.

"Yes, yes, I know all this," said Lung-Wang, his voice sounding bored. "My sister Kuang-li, the dragon who enlarges good, and my brother Kuang-jun, the dragon who enlarges favor, have told me all about you when we flew together in the night. I expected you long before this. You must have slept on the way."

"Never," said One Ox.

"Never," Two Ox said.

"Do not lie to me," said the Dragon King.

"We slept," they admitted.

"Good, good," the Dragon King murmured, his voice like water over stone. "And what pieces of magic have you for me? Not that tiresome folded pony of my sister's? It always returns home to her. And not that silly silver hairpin of my brother's. The waters only flow downhill." He twisted the ring once more around his finger, then polished it on his robe.

The two brothers held up the disfavored gifts. "Alas, they are all we have."

The Dragon King took the gifts and, putting his head back, roared with laughter. The sound filled the cave until the two brothers had to put their hands over their ears or be drowned in it.

Lung-Wang threw down the gifts at their feet and stopped laughing. In the sudden silence, the silver pin made a little tinkling noise on the rock floor and the packet whinnied painfully.

"Well, my two fine fellows, if this is all you have, then your mother will surely die."

They were about to answer him, to tell him about their brother Three Ox and the *wang-liang*'s face, when invisible fingers touched their lips and an invisible mouth whispered into their ears. "Trust no one else."

"What did you say?" the Dragon King asked suspiciously.

"Nothing, O great and mighty Lung-Wang," said One Ox.

"We just sighed," said Two Ox.

"Just so, just so," said Lung-Wang. "But if I ever suspect that you have lied to me, it will not go well with you. Since you have nothing more to offer me, you shall sit in my dungeon until I am ready to eat you. Perhaps at the end of this night. Or the next. Or even the one after that. The mountain climb has toughened you—but I like my meat that way. I am in no hurry; after all, dragons live a very long time." He picked them up by the back of their shirts as if they weighed no more than chicks and raised them until their heads nearly touched the roof. They were sure they could hear the sound of his great tail sweeping along behind.

The Dragon King's dungeon was of rock and stone and so far beneath the ground it was lit only by the phosphorescence in the rock. There was no need for bars on the door, for the door was but a hole in the roof high above them, down which they had been flung. When the brothers looked up, they could not see the hole for the dark.

"Three Ox, brother," they called up at last, "can you help us?"

"I will help, brothers," he called back down, "when I can. And see what I have in my hand."

"We can see nothing in the dark, brother," said One Ox.

"And even if we could," Two Ox added, "what you hold in your invisible hand becomes invisible itself."

"Just so," replied Three Ox. "Then I shall tell you. I have both the pocket beast and the pin."

"And what will you do now?" the brothers called up to him.

141

"What must be done," he answered, and was gone.

While One Ox and Two Ox waited in the cold and dark of their stone prison, Three Ox made his way back along the twisting tunnels of the cave, following the path swept clean by the dragon's tail. At last he found himself in a great room whose ceiling was lined with panels of obsidian and jade and whose walls were encrusted with pearl. In the center stood Lung-Wang, now more dragon than man. His shoulders, as green as the jade, were fiercely scaled; his eyes and teeth were the black of jet; and down from his back ran a sinuous, twisting green tail. But his hands were still a man's, and as the invisible boy watched, the Dragon King removed the ring from his own finger, reciting this charm:

Ring of power, ring of life,
Ring that neither blade nor knife
Nor ax nor sword can sever from me,
Swallow now so I become me!

Then the Dragon King threw the ring into the air and opened his mighty jaws to receive it.

In the second that the ring was thrown into the air, Three Ox remembered what the doctor had said. The ring was the guardian of the Waters of Life. It was also—clearly—the guardian of the Dragon King. He could not be transformed back into a man without it. Even as the ring was tumbling back down, the transformation into the King of all Dragons was complete.

Three Ox ran forward and leaped high into the air. With his invisible hand he snatched the ring before it could fall into the dragon's waiting jaws. Then in one swift, silent movement, he dived, somersaulted, and stood again, the ring now invisible in his closed hand.

For a moment more the Dragon King waited for the ring to fall into his open mouth. When it did not, he snapped his jaws shut with a sound as resounding as an executioner's ax.

"Where is it?" he cried. "Where is the Dragon King's own ring?" Falling on all fours, he began to sniff and snort and root around the room, lighting every crack and crevice with his fiery breath.

Three Ox did not wait for the Dragon King's search to be over. Swiftly and silently he made his way down the tunnels to the dungeon. There he stripped off his shirt and dangled it through the hole that served as the dungeon door. As the shirt was no longer on his body, it was visible to the point where it met his hand.

"Quickly, my brothers," he called, "grab hold of the shirt and I will pull you up. We have little time. Soon the dragon will stop searching for the ring alone and follow my scent."

But the shirt did not reach far enough down into the hole to help. So One Ox put Two Ox on his shoulders and then Two Ox was able to reach the shirt. With a mighty effort, Three Ox pulled him up. Then Two Ox took off his own shirt and tied it to Three Ox's. This way they had a long enough line to reach One Ox and pull him to safety. Then hand in hand in invisible hand they ran out of the cave.

Once outside, Three Ox stripped off the *wang-liang*'s face and held up the ring. "Here is the very thing that contains the Waters of Life. But unless we can escape the anger of the Dragon King we will not be able to bring it to our mother." He pulled the hairpin from his waistband. "Two Ox, you must get us down the mountainside with your river and boat."

"Gladly," said Two Ox, drawing the pin along the path. As he did so, a river began to bubble before them and there was the boat, bobbing gently in the current. "Climb in, my brothers, and I will bring us to the mountain's foot."

143

They climbed in, and using the silver pin as a rudder, Two Ox steered them with great skill down the steep mountainside. Behind them they heard the sound of a dragon roaring.

When they came to the bottom of the mountainside, the river stopped and so did the boat. They climbed out and Two Ox quickly took the rudder from the lock so that the boat and river became a pin once more. Then he stuck the pin in his waistband.

There was a full moon overhead and in the cool of the night all three boys shuddered.

"What now?" Two Ox asked.

"Now we must ride more swiftly than the dragon flies," Three Ox said, handing the packet to One Ox. "If we keep to the trees, we will be safe."

One Ox placed the packet on the ground. Then he unfolded it one piece at a time. As they watched, the horse grew and grew until it was large enough for three. They got on, One Ox in front, his fingers threaded through the horse's foam-colored mane. Behind him sat Two Ox, his arms around his brother's waist. And at the back sat Three Ox, clutching his brother's shirt.

The horse galloped swiftly beneath the trees all the night through, and so long as they remained hidden under the leafy boughs, the dragon could not get to them. But soon there lay ahead of them only farmland, and their mother's poor farm on the farther side.

"What can we do now?" asked One Ox.

"Dismount, my brothers," said Three Ox.

"How will that help?" asked Two Ox.

"I alone will ride to the farm, with the *wang-liang*'s face over my own, invisible. All the dragon will know is that a horse gallops swiftly below him. But you, my brothers, will not be riding." And as he spoke, he drew the *wang-liang*'s face down over his own. In a moment he could not be seen.

One Ox and Two Ox dismounted and hid themselves behind the largest tree at the forest's edge. As they watched, the horse shrank to fit a single rider, then pounded across the furrowed fields, heading straight toward their mother's farm. But the rider and part of the horse's back and mane could not be seen.

The dragon strained across the lightening sky, and when it saw the strange riderless horse, its anger was renewed. It pursued the horse with hot fury and hotter breath and soon flames singed the horse's tail. Still the horse galloped on and on; if anything, fire added to its speed. Within minutes it was at the farmhouse where the mother of One Ox, Two Ox, and Three Ox lay dying.

Hearing the commotion, the old woman tottered out of bed. And when she looked out into the growing dawn, she saw a horse galloping toward her with a great jade dragon behind it. She put her hand to her heart and cried out, "My son!" for though Three Ox was invisible to everyone else, he could not fool his mother's eyes.

Then the Dragon King understood how he had been deceived, and like a stooping hawk he cleaved his great jade wings to his sides and dived toward the running horse.

Just then the sun rose full over the farthest mountains, and its red eye burned into the dragon's jet eyes. The Dragon King gave an awful cry, remembering only at that moment that he had to be home by dawn. Then he burst like a series of bright skyrockets in the air; the light of it was seen as far away as the city of Kai-lung and down into the depths of the Western Sea. The ashes settled over the entire farm more than a *li* in length.

One Ox and Two Ox ran from the sheltering trees and joined their mother and brother in a mighty embrace by the farmhouse door. Then they dipped the Dragon King's ring into a glass of clear spring water. When their mother drank it down, she felt well again. In fact she felt better than she had in years.

Once the new crop was planted, One Ox went off to the city of Kai-lung to serve his dragon master for a year. And Two Ox went off to the Western Sea to serve his. But Three Ox stayed home to take care of his mother and tend the farm.

The farm flourished as never before because the ashes of the Dragon King made the soil rich and strong. When the two older brothers returned, there was more than enough for them all.

"Which is just as well," said their mother, "for I could never choose among my dear sons. I love each of you the best."

And indeed she did. For many years to come she played in the flowering orchards with her many grandchildren, giving them rides on the pocket pony, or floating with them in the silver boat, where she told them story after story after story just like the one I have just told you.

The old sailing maps, brittle and brown and decorated with pictures of spouting whales and leaping dolphins and a variety of sea serpents, have always fascinated me. Usually somewhere on those maps is the warning HERE THERE BE DRAGONS.

The places where such warnings were written tended to be dangerous spots in the ocean where ships had disappeared. Some may have been lost to sudden storms. Others to terrible tides. Still others to unlikely and hidden reefs. Or they may have been places where a volcanic island—like Surtsey near Iceland—suddenly rose in eruptions of flame and spouted rocks. I know something about Surtsey, having written about it in my book The Wizard Islands. *If I had been a sailor in the days before such underwater volcanic activity was understood, I might have mistaken it for a sea dragon.*

This poem, written on a gray April day in Massachusetts, with the rain sputtering down, muses on all of that.

Here There Be Dragons

The map tells sailors where to sail.
The decorations: sun and whale,
The warning spelled in letters pale:
  HERE THERE BE DRAGONS!

The well-known routes upon the map
Should cause the sailors no mishap,
But north-northwest there is a gap:
  AND HERE THERE BE DRAGONS!

The continents are not drawn true,
The ocean waves outlined in blue,
Sea serpentine provides the clue
WHERE THERE BE DRAGONS.

Yet year by year the ships have passed
Through oceans wide and oceans vast,
And sailors stared atop the mast
FOR WHERE THERE BE DRAGONS.

No scales of blue and jaws of green
Are by these modern sailors seen.
Do you think that this might mean
HERE THERE BE NO MORE DRAGONS?

I'd like to hope, I'd like to pray
The dragons have just gone . . . away . . .
And will return some other day,
THEN HERE THERE WILL BE DRAGONS.

AGAIN.